DECISION AT BRANDYWINE

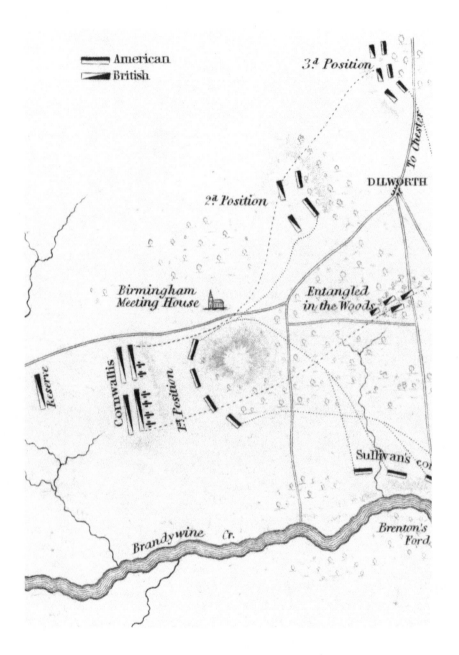

DECISION

AT

BRANDYWINE

The Battle on Birmingham Hill

ROBERT M. DUNKERLY

WESTHOLME
Yardley

Facing title page: Detail from a nineteenth-century map of the Battle of Brandywine showing the Birmingham Meeting House at center. (*New York Public Library*)

Westholme Publishing, LLC
904 Edgewood Road
Yardley, Pennsylvania 19067
Visit our Web site at www.westholmepublishing.com

ISBN: 978-1-59416-366-1
Also available as an eBook

Printed in the United States of America

CONTENTS

Maps

Birmingham Hill on the Brandywine battlefield at dawn. Photograph by Meredith Barnes. (©Molly Picture Studio)

PREFACE

BRANDYWINE HAS FASCINATED ME SINCE I WAS YOUNG. I remember writing a report on it in elementary school. (Okay, my dad helped. A lot.) My first visit was with family and I was enamored, taking an excessive number of photos and exploring every corner where I could convince my parents to stop. I remember dodging traffic on Route 1 to get a photo I just had to have, perhaps the start of a habit I still practice.

I returned again after many years while working as a seasonal park ranger in Virginia, at the start of my career in history. Visiting the park's museum and taking the driving tour reignited my interest in the battle. I appreciated how it was one of the largest of the war. I understood Brandywine, Germantown, and Valley Forge as critical periods of the war, a time when the Continental Army was well established and fighting major battles against the British.

A few years later another visit in the early 2000s brought me at a time when I was intensely interested in the development of the Continental Army and had done much study on military tactics and drill manuals. These factors, I felt, were key to how combat unfolded and to understanding battles of the period. I came to see Brandywine in a new light. This battle was extremely important in the evolution of the Continental Army and it seemed that it was not widely appreciated as such.

I also grasped that the fighting on Birmingham Hill was not only the center of the battlefield but the real area of fighting—the heart of the battlefield. There was combat elsewhere, but this is where the two sides slugged it out and where the battle was decided. Not only was this fact not widely appreciated but this part of the battlefield was not preserved or publicly accessible.

Despite that obstacle, I began to study the battle in detail and began working on a research project that has evolved into the book you hold in your hands. My initial thinking was that lack of a uniform drill manual (for marching, fighting, and maneuvering) would be my central theme. In time I modified this stance, but I still feel it is a crucial point. As I studied this and other battles and reflected more deeply, I came to see Brandywine as the first major battle of this scale for many of the Continental troops, and my focus shifted to emphasizing the importance of that. Comparing Brandywine to other battles and comparing the deployment and experience of these troops put this battle into its proper context.

In the meantime great strides had been made by the late 2010s to preserve more of the site, and more areas are now saved for posterity, with additional gains on the horizon. In fact, compared to the previous decades of inaction and neglect, the last few years have seen a rapid acceleration in preserving and interpreting the battlefield.

In researching this work, I have driven every road in the core battlefield area, walked every publicly accessible acre, and visited every monument and marker at the site (sometimes at great risk to my safety!). I also insisted on understanding the battle from the soldier's perspective, after all that was what I was writing about, and I wanted to see and experience what I was claiming to understand. That effort culminated in hiking the route of the fifteen-mile British flank march on a spring day with one of my best friends who graciously agreed to go through the experience with me. (Thanks, Tom!) Unlike for the British in 1777, we had cold beers waiting for us at the end, but walking the very ground and studying the terrain was invaluable.

I think that Brandywine has much to teach us, and we have much to learn about it. I hope we never stop digging or learning and preserving.

INTRODUCTION

"The grandest scene I ever saw, a sight beyond description"
—Major Joseph Bloomfield, 3rd New Jersey

THE BATTLE OF BRANDYWINE, FOUGHT SEPTEMBER 11, 1777, was one of the largest battles of the Revolutionary War, yet it has had few detailed studies. Nor has there been a meticulous analysis of the fighting on Birmingham Hill near the Quaker Birmingham Meeting House. This was the heart of the battlefield and saw the most vicious fighting that day.

The Continental and British armies, under Generals George Washington and William Howe respectively, had maneuvered and skirmished for several days. Howe intended to capture the American capital of Philadelphia; Washington was determined to prevent it. Although fighting occurred throughout the day and over ten square miles, it was the action for about an hour on Birmingham Hill that determined the day's outcome.

Focusing on only one part of the battlefield might seem odd for a Revolutionary War site, but it is not uncommon in military history. Battlefields are often broken down into areas for detailed study: there are numerous works on Gettysburg's Wheat Field, Devils' Den, or Pickett's Charge; Antietam's Sunken Road; or Shiloh's Hornet's Nest. Any battlefield has those key areas where fighting was concentrated or events were crucial to the overall outcome. Birmingham Hill was that crucial spot for Brandywine.

Brandywine was fought when the Continental Army was still developing. Author Herman Benninghoff II writes in his book, *Valley Forge: A Genesis of Command, Continental Army Style*, that "The Battle of Brandywine was an American defeat, demonstrating the lack of an effective command and control process, which contributed to an uncoordinated performance of operating units."[1]

Historian John Trussell, an authority on the Revolution in Pennsylvania, agrees, noting that,

> One of the major defects of the American army up to the time it reached Valley Forge had been that, to the extent that the troops had been taught any formations and maneuvers, they had been trained on wildly divergent lines. Each state had its own preferences with regard to military doctrine. The units of some states had been trained on the British pattern, others on the French, and still others on the Prussian. This diversity was serious, since infantry tactics of that period . . . were based on close-order drill. Without a standard system, cohesive teamwork on the battlefield was almost impossible to attain.[2]

In one example he notes that "the length of the step and the cadence varied from one regiment to the next." These differences made coordination difficult, especially under combat conditions.[3]

Brandywine was an important engagement and has only recently received detailed examination by scholars. It was the first major battle at the start of a crucial campaign, one that very well could have ended the war. It is unfortunate that the battle has not received more attention or has not been better preserved.

It was the first major battle for the new version of the Continental Army formed that spring. Units had arrived in New Jersey that spring of 1777 and fought in small engagements, often against

British foraging parties. Yet not until Brandywine in September did the entire army fight a large battle. Brandywine was their first major test.

Brandywine was the second largest engagement of the war, behind Monmouth, in terms of numbers engaged (over thirty thousand). Lastly, Brandywine was the third bloodiest fight of the war, after Camden and Germantown, with 1,300 American and 581 British casualties, for a total of 1,881.[4]

To those who fought in this massive engagement, spread out over ten square miles and lasting from late afternoon until dark, it was unforgettable. It truly must have been, as Major Joseph Bloomfield said, "the grandest scene I ever saw, a sight beyond description."[5]

It is hoped that the detailed study of the fighting on Birmingham Hill adds to our knowledge of the heart of the battle, as well as to Revolutionary War combat in general. Crucial to an analysis of the actions at Birmingham Hill is an understanding of the Continental Army's lack of uniform training and experience. Training is important before any army takes the field, and the Continental Army's lack of a uniform drill manual—combined with a lack of experience fighting in large, open-field battles—played a major role in their defeat at Brandywine. This study examines the army's training and capability—up to September 11, 1777—and dissects the battle on Birmingham Hill in minute detail, offering a case study in weapons, tactics, and terrain analysis critical to a holistic understanding of Washington's defeat and what it would mean for the future of the Continental Army.

A plate from William Windham's *A Plan for Discipline Composed for the Use of Militia of the County of Norfolk* to which was added "The manual exercise, with explanations, as ordered by His Majesty," London: J. Millan, 1766. This illustration is part of a series that accompanied the Norfolk Discipline. Here the soldier is moving the musket to his left side, which is where troops carried the weapon when marching. This is one example of the many drill manuals used by the armies at this time.

Chapter 1

COMMAND
AND
CONTROL
AND
LINEAR COMBAT

"Time in which to become Soldiers"
—General Carl von Donop

An understanding of eighteenth-century linear combat is essential to appreciate the significance of the fighting on Birmingham Hill. How armies fight—in any century—is largely dictated by weapons and terrain. Those two factors influence tactics, the details of how armies deploy and engage.

The standard military weapon of the day was a smoothbore flintlock musket. Smoothbore meant that there was no rifling in the barrel, making it easier to load, but less accurate, than a rifle. The flintlock was the ignition system: a piece of flint struck a piece of steel, creating a spark to ignite the gunpowder.

The weapons required several steps to load, and various manuals were developed to outline the steps. They included tearing open a paper cartridge with the teeth, pouring a little powder into the pan of the musket, inserting the wad (with lead ball) down the barrel, ramming it, replacing the ramrod, and cocking the weapon to fire it.

These muskets, whether they were French Charleville or British Brown Bess (Short or Long Land Pattern) were accurate up to about a hundred yards. Soldiers could load and fire about two to three times a minute, depending on their training and battlefield conditions. The rate of fire decreased over time, due to weapons being fouled by black powder in the barrels, position adjustments, distractions from incoming fire, and other variables.

Combat followed a predictable pattern of load, volley, and reload. Due to the range of the weapons, troops were massed to maximize their effectiveness, creating a volley to inflict maximum casualties. Troops also had to be in range of their enemy, thus fighting was generally at less than a hundred yards, sometimes much less.

Under such stressful conditions—close formations, the rigorous loading process, the close quarters with the enemy—discipline was crucial. Armies had to have a command and control system to regulate the movement of troops and their functions on the battlefield.

Discipline, morale, and control were all key. So was consistency. A drill manual had to be followed precisely or troops could not fight effectively. Manuals spelled out the steps for loading and firing, dictated marching pace, and oversaw how troops formed a battle line from a marching column and how they maneuvered. For example, the command in the British Manual of 1764 to pick up and carry the weapon was "Shoulder Your Firelock!" but in another manual it was something else. So were the steps to handle the weapon, moving it from the ground to the soldier's side. This was also true of loading and firing: different steps with different commands.

The British troops in General Howe's army were following the British Manual of 1764, with some modifications for combat in

Top: British Pattern 1769 Short Land "Brown Bess" musket. Used throughout the eighteenth century, in 1768 the British military introduced a version that was six inches shorter than the original model. This newer version became known as the Short Land Pattern, and the earlier version the Long Land Pattern. Both were used by the British army, as well as the Americans. (*Museum of American History/Smithsonian*) Bottom: A firing line. Troops stood shoulder to shoulder in line to load and fire at the enemy. This type of combat took training and discipline. (*Author*)

America. The Hessians were following their own manual. Yet the various American units they faced used an assortment of manuals.

The units from various states, having never trained together before, used different manuals. Examples include Humphrey Bland's *Treatise on Military Discipline*, William Windham's *A Plan for Discipline Composed for the Use of Militia of the County of Norfolk*, Timothy Pickering's *An Easy Plan for Discipline for Militia*, and the British Manual of 1764.

They all differed in the number of steps, the name of the commands, and the physical process of loading, firing, marching, and maneuvering. Later at Valley Forge in March 1778, Washington noted that he saw three brigades use different manuals, and the result was a lack of coordination. Upon assuming his role at the encampment, General Friedrich Wilhelm August Heinrich Ferdinand von Steuben simplified the commands and created one common drill for the entire army.[1]

Troops from Massachusetts used Bland's manual, while the Norfolk Discipline was widely used by other New England units. Probably the most commonly used manual in the other states was the British 1764 Manual, since, as British colonies, British military drill would have been used by colonial militias in the prewar years. When the states organized their military forces at the start of the Revolution, this was the drill they knew. There were likely other variations in the training disciplines used among the states and within regions of states.[2]

Washington himself favored Bland, recommending it to Virginia officers for use in their training in the fall of 1775. How widespread this manual became among those units is unknown.[3]

Just prior to the outbreak of the war, Virginia, Connecticut, and North Carolina officially adopted the 1764 Manual for their troops. Like many other prewar militias, New Jersey troops used the British 1764 Manual, and this continued when the conflict started.[4]

The other challenge facing the Americans was the fact that these units, some of them new to combat, had not fought together in such a large formation in an open field battle. The timing for various movements would have been off, and different units would have executed certain actions differently. The variations could be important, especially in the tense situation of actual combat when timing and coordination are crucial. The manuals used different commands for the loading and firing process, as well as how to maneuver and change positioning. The differences included not only the command words but the physical steps to loading and carrying the weapon, as well as how troops formed and marched.

Portrait of George Washington by Charles Willson Peale, 1776. George Washington had extensive experience leading small units from the French and Indian War, and understood the deficiencies of his army in 1777. Pressing issues kept him from being able to address the army's training until the winter at Valley Forge. (*White House Collection*)

Although the Continental Army had been in the field for two years, state and regional rivalries were intense, and there had been little effort to unify the systems on which the army operated. Of course, this happened later at Valley Forge, when "one system of Discipline and Tacticks" was adopted. But that was in the future, and as British and Hessian troops were bearing down on American troops (from five different states and Canada), attempting to form and coordinate among themselves was a challenge.[5]

General George Weedon, whose troops were engaged late in the action at Brandywine, wrote later at Valley Forge that "to practice a Single manoever" was crucial. He noted, "Any alteration or Inovation, will again plunge the army into that contrariety and confusion, from which it is endeavouring to emerge."[6]

Washington and other officers were not blind to the problem. The commander in chief wrote in May 1777 to General Alexander MacDougall, "I agree perfectly with you in the impropriety of that diversity in the modes of training our Regiments which has prevailed hereto. I have it in contemplation, very soon to digest and establish a regular system of discipline, manoeuvers, evolutions, regulations for guard, etc. to be observed throughout the Army."[7]

Unable to address the issue at the time, he recommended that MacDougall "introduce an uniformity among those you command," emphasizing training to "enable them to perform the necessary movement in marching and forming with ease, order agility and expedition."[8]

Noteworthy is Washington's emphasis on not the details of loading and firing but on formations and maneuvering, which were crucial on the battlefield. Large units had to be able to maneuver and cooperate, with all of their components in tandem. The Continental units had never fought in large units and formations in a big open field battle of the size and scale of Brandywine, and the diverse training and drill would hamper them this day.

In 1775 at the start of the conflict, General Washington noted the need for discipline and uniformity in the army. Its training, equipment, and uniforms had to be standardized. He wrote of the need for a "Respectable Army." The grueling campaigns of 1776, combined with short enlistments, lack of supplies, and flagging public support for the army, made achieving that goal out of reach. Yet it never left Washington's mind and he continued to advocate for the reforms he needed.

In combat, troops deployed into a line of battle two ranks deep. Each soldier occupied about two feet of space. Thus 1,000 men deployed into a two-rank battle line occupied about 333 yards (1,000 feet) of space, with 500 in each rank (front and rear).

On paper an American infantry regiment's strength was 720 men, yet even before units reached the field they were already under strength. Illness, transfers to other units, desertion, and detached assignments lowered effective numbers even before battle. Especially for the units that had fought in the New York and New Jersey

Continental major generals John Sullivan, left, and William Alexander (Lord Stirling) right. Anxious to clear his name after the defeat, Sullivan wrote at length defending his actions at Birmingham Hill. He likely did the best he could under the circumstances. Stirling was an experienced division commander who served Washington faithfully through the whole war. Captured at Long Island and then exchanged, he commanded the troops who fought at Short Hills, New Jersey, prior to Brandywine. (*Library of Congress; New York Public Library*)

campaigns, losses had been high and numbers were well down. The average American regimental strength at Brandywine was about 169 men.[9]

Three divisions of Washington's army fought in the action at Birmingham Hill, commanded by Major Generals William Alexander (Lord Stirling), Adam Stephen, and John Sullivan. As the senior commander, Sullivan assumed command of the entire force, and so, in the absence of Brigadier General William Smallwood, French General de Borre advanced from brigade to temporary division command that afternoon. Smallwood had been sent back to Maryland to recruit and missed the battle.

Of the twenty-six American units in the fighting on Birmingham Hill, the eight Maryland regiments never properly deployed. Of the remaining eighteen that were engaged, only the strength of some are known. The largest regiment on the hill that day was likely the 2nd Canadian with 400, followed by the 11th Virginia with 377 men, and the 2nd and 3rd New Jersey each had about 300 men. Some regiments had 100 to 150 men; the Delaware Regiment had only 79.

General Adam Stephen's division was the largest present for this fight and in fact the second largest in the army, at nearly 2,000 men. Stirling could bring 1,800 to bear from his division and Sullivan about 1,700 from his. Facing them would be a British/German strength of about 9,000 men—all veteran troops—an almost two-to-one advantage.[10]

Brandywine was also the first fight for the reorganized Continental Army. By now it had gone through two transformations. General Washington inherited a largely New England militia force in the spring of 1775 around Boston. The next year, most state designations were abolished and regiments were numbered as Continental infantry, from one to twenty-six. This army was enlisted for one year and gained valuable experience in the New York and New Jersey campaigns.

After Trenton and Princeton, Washington successfully persuaded Congress that longer enlistments were needed, and states began to organize more regiments. The old Continental units' terms of service expired, and they were replaced by those from state quotas. This new army first took the field as a large, unified force at Brandywine. While some were veterans from the previous two years, many were not. More importantly, the units had not yet served together on a large scale.

The Continental troops who fought on Birmingham Hill were from Virginia, Maryland, Delaware, New Jersey, Pennsylvania, and Canada. Most had prior combat experience but little training in complex maneuvering. The British and German troops opposing them were veterans, and General Howe led the attack with his elite: the Brigade of Guards, Grenadiers, Light Infantry, and Jaegers. (For more details on the units, their experience, and capabilities, see Appendix A.)

Chapter 2

THE BATTLE OF BRANDYWINE UNFOLDS

"At Daybreak the army marched in two columns."
—Corporal Thomas Sullivan, 49th British Regiment

BRANDYWINE WOULD BE THE FIRST MAJOR BATTLE for the reorganized Continental Army of 1777. Contemporaries referred to the army directly under Washington's control, operating in the mid-Atlantic, as the main army, to differentiate it from other armies in upstate New York and the Carolinas. At the end of 1776 many of the main army's existing regiments' terms of enlistment expired, and Congress authorized the raising of new regiments.

Whereas most of the old units from 1775 had been designated as "Continental" regiments, the ones formed after the close of 1776 were named after their state. As these new units joined the army near Morristown in the spring of 1777, they began to skirmish with British forces in northern central New Jersey, but even the largest, like Short Hills and Bound Brook, only involved regiments or brigades at most, not entire divisions. Thus they had little or no experience maneuvering or fighting as large units or coordinating with other units.

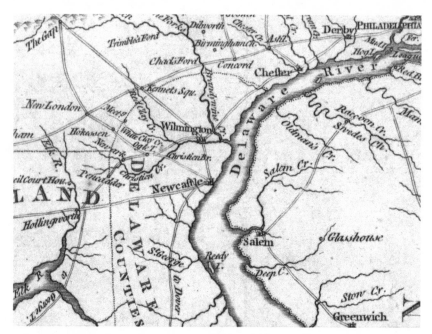

Detail from "Seat of War in the environs of Philadelphia," London, 1777. The Elk River is at bottom left. Wilmington, Delaware, is about center, with Kennett Square and Chad's Ford above. Philadelphia is at upper right. (*New York Public Libary*)

The 1777 campaign season opened promisingly for the British in North America. Having already secured New York City, a British force descended from Canada down the Hudson corridor while another, the army under General William Howe, landed in the Chesapeake and moved toward Philadelphia. Leadership in London expected Howe to coordinate with General John Burgoyne's army coming from Canada, however, the order never reached Howe. Thus the two main British thrusts of 1777 went forward without coordination.

Using their naval superiority, Admiral Richard Howe moved his brother's army by water from New York City to the Chesapeake Bay. The British began unloading on August 25 at Turkey Point, Maryland, below Head of Elk (between modern Elkton and North East).

The monument to the action at Cooch's Bridge, flanked by Civil War-era cannons, stands just yards away from the site of the old bridge. Cooch's Bridge was the only Revolutionary War battle fought in Delaware. The bridge stood to the right, just out of this picture. (*Author*)

Aware that the British were on the move but unsure of their intentions, General Washington had to wait until he had confirmation of their location. The Continental Army had moved from New Jersey to the Germantown area, just north of Philadelphia. With word of Howe's arrival at Head of Elk, Washington reacted quickly. The Continental Army marched through Philadelphia toward Maryland and Delaware.

In the meantime the British advanced east from Head of Elk into Delaware, reaching Aiken's Tavern. The only battle to occur in the state took place on September 3, as American troops slowed the British and German advance on the west side of Cooch's Bridge, below Newark.

Howe then moved his army north, passing through Newark and Hockessin, arriving at New Garden, Pennsylvania. The British then

A portrait of British General Sir William Howe, 5th Viscount Howe, published in November 1777. Commanding all British forces in North America, Howe personally led the campaign to capture Philadelphia. Howe was a political moderate who was sympathetic to the Americans. (*Anne S. K. Military Collection, Brown University*)

moved to Kennett Square. Washington initially blocked Wilmington and then shifted north as the British did, arriving at Chad's Ford.

By September 10 Washington took up a defensive position on the eastern side of the Brandywine River, blocking the main road to Philadelphia (the Post Road, now US 1). General Howe's army was just five miles away at Kennett Square. The most direct approach for the British was on the Post Road, which ran from Kennett Square to Chad's Ford, and it was here that Washington concentrated his army.

The area encompassing the battlefield had several important landmarks, including the Post Road, running east to west and crossing the river at Chad's Ford. Washington concentrated his army to block a river crossing here as well as the nearby fords above it. His headquarters at the Ring House was about a mile and a half east of Chad's Ford.

Deployed parallel to the river, roughly north-south, were the divisions of Stephen, Sullivan, and Stirling. They guarded the river crossings north of Chad's: Brinton's Ford, Jones's Ford, Wistar's Ford, and Buffington's Ford. To the south of Chad's Ford the Pennsylvania militia deployed to block any river crossing.

Immediately north of the Post Road the ground was wooded and hilly with steep slopes and cut by several creeks. Farther north and east the ground was more open and suitable for maneuver. Here Sandy Hollow, Birmingham Hill, and Osborne's Hill were generally open and rolling, broken by fences, woodlots, and orchards.

Farther to the east, running roughly north to south, was the Wilmington Road. The core of the battlefield, where most of the fighting occurred, can roughly be said to be bordered on the west by the Brandywine River, on the south by the Post Road, the north by Street Road, and the east by the Wilmington Road.

Events began early on the morning of September 11. General Howe's army consisted of two divisions: one under Lieutenant General Charles Cornwallis and another led by Lieutenant General Wilhelm von Knyphausen. Sending Knyphausen's division forward against the American position along the river as a distraction, Howe accompanied Cornwallis's troops on a twelve-mile march around the Americans' position to outflank the enemy.

These troops began marching around 5 a.m. and successfully got around the American army undetected. Howe had surprised Washington again, moving his army around the Americans as he had done earlier at Long Island and White Plains. Throughout the day Washington received conflicting information about a possible British flank attack, but it was not conclusive.

Advancing east toward Chad's Ford along the Post Road,

Overleaf: Howe's Battle Plan: The British Flanking March. Moving about fifteen miles, the British and German troops of Cornwallis' division emerged behind the American army. (From Michael Harris, *Battle of Brandywine*, p. 218. Used with permission.)

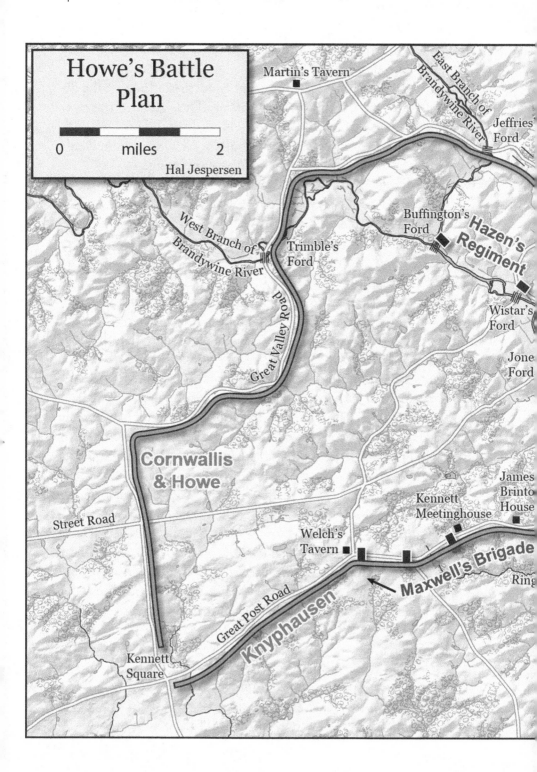

Howe's Battle Plan

0 miles 2

Hal Jespersen

Martin's Tavern

East Branch of Brandywine River

Jeffries Ford

West Branch of Brandywine River

Trimble's Ford

Buffington's Ford

Hazen's Regiment

Wistar's Ford

Great Valley Road

Jone Ford

Cornwallis & Howe

James Brinto House

Kennett Meetinghouse

Street Road

Welch's Tavern

Maxwell's Brigade

Ring

Knyphausen

Great Post Road

Kennett Square

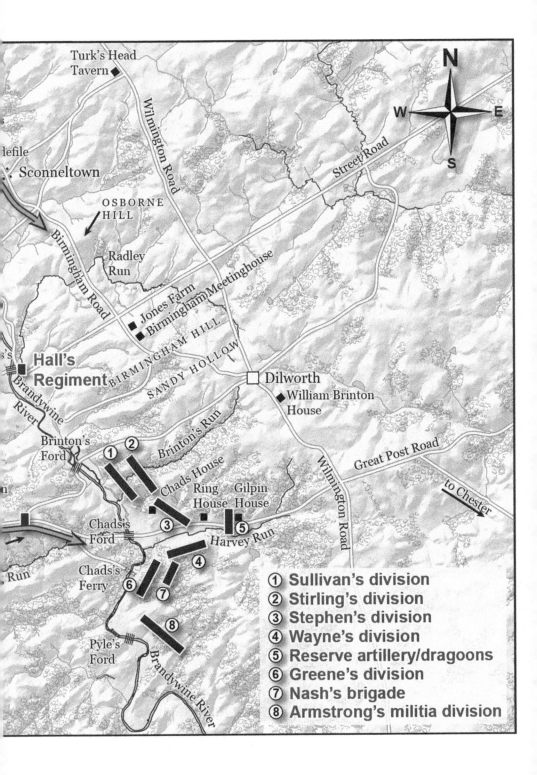

Turk's Head
Tavern

N

W E

S

Sconneltown

lefile

Wilmington Road

Street Road

OSBORNE
HILL

Radley
Run

Birmingham Road

Jones Farm

Birmingham Meetinghouse

BIRMINGHAM HILL

SANDY HOLLOW

Dilworth

William Brinton
House

Hall's
Regiment

Brandywine
River

Brinton's
Ford

Brinton's Run

Chads House

Ring
House

Gilpin
House

Great Post Road

to Chester

Wilmington Road

Chads's
Ford

Harvey Run

Chads's
Ferry

Run

Pyle's
Ford

Brandywine River

① **Sullivan's division**
② **Stirling's division**
③ **Stephen's division**
④ **Wayne's division**
⑤ **Reserve artillery/dragoons**
⑥ **Greene's division**
⑦ **Nash's brigade**
⑧ **Armstrong's militia division**

Washington's Headquarters. The commanding general occupied the Ring House, just east of Chad's Ford along the Post Road. The house was reconstructed on its original foundation, and is part of the Brandywine Battlefield State Historic Site. It is open for tours seasonally. (*Author*)

Knyphausen engaged the newly formed Light Infantry force under General William Maxwell. The Continental troops on the west side of the creek intended to slow down the enemy advance toward Chad's Ford. They made several stands at Welch's Tavern, Kennett Meeting House, and the James Brinton House before falling back and crossing the river.

Knyphausen's German and British troops then deployed along the west bank of the river, occupying Washington's attention as intended. Still concerned about a possible flank attack, Washington waited and then decided that he should strike at the enemy and ordered an assault. Before that could be implemented, however, events changed rapidly.

Shortly after 2:00 p.m., Washington had definite confirmation that his force was being turned and his army was in trouble. He

Upon reaching this high ground at Osborne Hill, General Howe's column took a break from their long march. British and German troops spread out here to eat their rations and rest from the march. Here local civilian Joseph Townsend wandered among the troops. (*Author*)

quickly dispatched orders for General William Alexander, Lord Stirling, to move his and the division of General Adam Stephen to meet the attack. He then sent General John Sullivan with his division and orders to oversee all three. General Nathanael Greene was also readied to bring up his division. This left General Anthony Wayne's division of Pennsylvania Continentals and the Pennsylvania Militia under General John Armstrong to hold the position at Chad's Ford opposite Knyphausen's troops.

In the meantime, the column under Howe and Cornwallis had crossed the Brandywine at the unguarded Jefferis Ford and turned south. Their route would take them over Osborne Hill and Birmingham Hill into the very back of the American army. The Continental troops would have to react quickly and efficiently to meet the threat.

The Americans may have been flanked, but the British needed to take a break from their long trek, which gave the Americans a chance to even the odds. Having marched twelve miles in the September heat, the British and German troops needed a rest. General Howe ordered his men to break ranks and eat their rations on Osborne Hill, which rises north of Street Road. Stirling's and Stephen's divisions arrived from the south and took position on a prominent hill facing the British troops, about a mile and a half to the south. This was Birmingham Hill, sometimes also called the Plowed Hill.

Joseph Townsend, a twenty-one-year-old Quaker resident, saw the British marching by and followed them on their march toward Osborne Hill, "possessed of curiosity." Other civilians turned out as well to see the spectacle. They had never seen anything like it before: nine thousand marching men, colorful uniforms, and dozens of horses drawing artillery and wagons.[1]

After receiving permission to walk among the resting troops, Townsend moved freely through the British and German troops on Osborne Hill. He and his brother stopped to talk to several of them. Joseph recorded, "They inquired what sort of a man Mr. Washington was. My brother had a knowledge of him by being with him at his quarters at Chad's Ford, and replied that he was a stately, well proportioned, fine looking man, of great ability, active, firm, and resolute, of a social disposition, and was considered to be a good man." This description, he observed, was to check their ardour for a sight of him, and to bring forward some further observations from them respecting him, to which one of them answered "that he might be a good man, but he was most damnably misled to take up arms against his sovereign."[2]

In the meantime, Stirling's and Stephen's divisions arrived on Birmingham Hill and deployed. These troops had never been part of such a large formation. Stirling's division formed on the left, with Stephen on his right. Four American infantry brigades, with two batteries of artillery, readied for combat. The hill was an excellent defensive position, and the Americans had reached it fortuitously as the British were resting.

Sullivan came up last and began to form his men in what he thought was an extension of the American line. Instead, he realized that he was about half a mile to the left and in front of Stirling and Stephen. The gap must be closed, and fast, for the British were finishing their break and reforming and preparing to attack. Watching the Americans form, Howe ordered his army back into formation for the assault. From Sullivan's position he could not see the other two divisions, but he learned that they were separated. The British, from Osborne's Hill about half a mile away, could see the Americans arriving and deploying.

The movement of the Continental troops was made cross country and involved crossing hilly terrain. That Sullivan's division found the right place to deploy, lacking maps and never having seen this ground, was fortunate. As this unfolded, the Maryland brigades found themselves in a rapidly changing, fluid situation and were not able to adjust quickly or easily. Even though they were among the army's best units, the Maryland and Delaware troops struggled as the battle opened.

Good leadership is crucial in combat. Unfortunately some of the army's most experienced leaders, like William Maxwell (of the New Jersey brigade) and William Smallwood (of the Maryland troops), were either absent or on other parts of the field. There were several experienced European officers like the Frenchman Preudhomme de Borre and the Irish-born Frenchman Thomas Conway, yet they served here with mixed results. The Continental officers deploying their troops on Birmingham Hill around three o'clock that afternoon would be severely tested in the coming hour.

Birmingham Meeting House. Ironically this house of worship, used by pacifists, was at the center of the British attack at Brandywine. After the battle it served as a hospital for the wounded of both sides. (*Author*)

Chapter 3

THE BATTLE DEVELOPS AT BIRMINGHAM HILL

"The enemy came on with fury."
—Lieutenant Ebenezer Elmer, 3rd New Jersey

THIS AND THE NEXT TWO CHAPTERS examine in detail the combat on Birmingham Hill, analyzing the American and British units from east to west (the American left to their right, conversely the British right to their left). It is difficult to accurately establish time, as only a handful of accounts mention time, and time was relative based on one's watch settings. The events described happened swiftly and simultaneously and will be recounted as best as can be determined from existing accounts.

The land on which the fighting developed had been purchased only a year before by Jesse Graves, and his family's story is an example of the randomness, and cruelty, of war. Graves, his wife Elizabeth, and their children Susannah, Jehu, Tacy, and Hannah, were Quakers who moved onto the property in July 1776.

Jesse had purchased 184 acres, which included land on both sides of the Birmingham Road and the high ground just to the south of it. The family worshiped at the nearby meeting house, which bordered their property.

Following the battle, Graves reported his losses at the hands of the British: tools and clothing stolen and farm animals taken. The family lost heavily and moved away in 1783, the same year that the Treaty of Paris ended the war.[1]

Although fought two years into the war, and after large battles such as Long Island, White Plains, Trenton, and Princeton, Brandywine was actually the first large open-field battle. Most previous battles involved limited open field fighting, were fought with earthworks, or had involved fewer men. All of these factors make Brandywine an important case study for evaluating the evolution of warfare during the conflict.

Many American units here had not fought in the earlier large battles, having joined the army in the spring of 1777. Their first taste of combat was in central New Jersey with abundant skirmishing and smaller engagements. Yet Brandywine would be their first major battle.

Brandywine was a classic eighteenth-century linear battle, fought over fields and rolling hills. It was the kind of battle British and German troops were well versed in and that the Americans had not quite yet mastered. For the first time in the war, these American troops fought as divisions and brigades in open terrain. It must have been an impressive sight, one that would not be seen again until Monmouth the following summer.

Thus the scale of Brandywine makes it much larger than the engagements fought previously, where only regiments or parts of brigades had been engaged. Earlier battles at Long Island (brigades and regiments), Harlem Heights (regiments), White Plains (regiments), Ft. Washington (regiments), Trenton (brigades), and Princeton (regiments and brigades) had not involved these larger formations. Thus none of the American commanders on the field that day had exercised command and control on such a scale.

In addition, Washington himself had not commanded personally at Long Island, Harlem, or Ft. Washington. This would be one of the first major tests of his ability to maneuver and control an en-

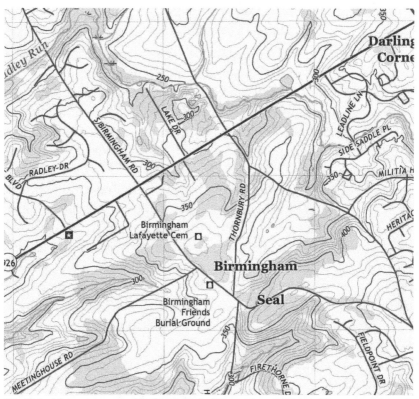

Geological Survey topographical map of the Birmingham Hill area. This map shows the terrain that impacted the fighting. Street Road runs diagonally across the map. The Birmingham Friends Burial Ground is actually across the road from where it is shown on this map; instead, this is where the Meetinghouse and Quaker cemetery are located. The American position was on the high ground near the "350" topo line, in the lower center. Note the ridges and valley shown by the topographic lines between Street Road and the American position. The heaviest fighting took place where the words "Birmingham Friends Burial Ground" are located.

tire army on the battlefield. It was, in fact, the largest battle he had yet personally commanded in his career.[2]

For the attack at Brandywine, British commander Howe divided his forces. One column, led by Lieutenant General Knyphausen, moved straight along the Great Post Road (now Route 1) to attack and distract the Americans. This movement was the most likely effort that Washington expected his enemy to make. In the meantime, General Charles Lord Cornwallis marched his division about seventeen miles to the north to swing around the Americans and attack from the flank. Howe himself accompanied this column.

Faulty intelligence plagued Washington all morning, with conflicting reports that the British were marching around his flank or not. Troops were deployed to block the fords of the river, and scouts were active that morning. Believing he finally understood the situation, around noon Washington ordered his troops to attack the British across the Brandywine River. Then word arrived that indeed the enemy had marched around to the right and was bearing down on his position. Immediately Washington canceled the attack and dispatched the divisions of Generals Alexander and Stephen north.

Local soldier Samuel White of Chester County recalled the battle years later, stating, "about three Oclock P.M. when we received orders to march to meet the enemy who we understood had crossed the Brandywine about nine miles above us, we met them at a rising piece of ground near a Quaker Meetinghouse called Bromage Meeting home when we immediately engaged them and sustained our position for about an hour when we were compelled to retreat. We lost a number of our men in the engagement and killed a great many of them." The Pennsylvania militia, to whom White belonged, was not engaged at Birmingham Meeting House, so he is referring to the army as a whole shifting and fighting there.[3]

General John Sullivan recounted that, as his division left their position at Britton's Ford, "I began my march a few minutes after I received my orders, and had not marched a mile when I met Colonel Hazen and his regiment, who informed me that the enemy were close upon his heels, and that I might depend that the main part of the British army were there."

Hazen's French Canadian troops (part of Sullivan's division) had been on the army's far right flank, guarding Wistar's Ford and Buffington's Ford on the Brandywine. They withdrew and met up with Sullivan as his troops were coming up from the south.

Sullivan wrote that he "ordered Colo. Hazens Regiment to pass a Hollow way, File off to the Right & face to Cover the Artillery while it was passing the Same Hollow way, the Rest of the Troops followed in the Rear to assist in Covering the Artillery the Enemy

Seeing this did not press on but gave me time to form my Division on an advantageous Heights in a Line with the other Divisions but almost half a mile to the Left.[4]

"While I was conversing with Colonel Hazen," Sullivan said further, "and our troops still upon the march, the enemy headed us in the road about forty rods from our advanced guard." Sullivan saw that he was too far to the left, separated from the other two divisions, and acted to unite his troops with them. Sullivan said, "I then found it necessary to turn off to the right and form."

The troops of Sullivan's division had arrived on a rise of ground just south of Street Road, south of its intersection with modern Eleni Lane. Looking around, Sullivan realized he was separated from the other two divisions of Stirling and Stephen by about a mile. The terrain is rolling and wooded, so he would not have had a clear view but perhaps had caught glimpses of the other troops on his ride up to this location. Sullivan rode over to meet with them and discuss their deployment. He later wrote that the British "gave me time to form on an advantageous height in a line with the other divisions, but almost a mile to the left."[5]

Consulting with Stirling and Stephen, Sullivan noted that they were all "unanimously of the opinion that my division should be brought on to join the others, and that the whole should incline further to the right to prevent our being outflanked . . ."[6]

Wasting no time, he ordered Stephen and Stirling to move to their right to make room for his brigades on Birmingham Hill. Sullivan then returned to his troops and instructed General de Borre to oversee the movement while he rode over to consult again with Stephen and Stirling.

De Borre ordered a maneuver that was too complicated, marching the division south from their exposed position, turning them east, and then wheeling them up to their intended place in the line of battle. Perhaps, in the heat of the moment, he felt this was the best course. Perhaps he was considering terrain obstacles that we are not aware of today.[7]

Colonel John Stone of the 1st Maryland Regiment, who was probably commanding the 1st Maryland Brigade (it is not clear

Street (Straight) Road, which existed at the time of the battle, ran east to west through a valley north of Birmingham Hill. The British and German units moved through here during their attack. This view looks south through the intersection of Street Road (running left to right) and Birmingham Road. The British Light Infantry and Grenadiers advanced here, followed by the Fourth Brigade. (*Author*)

who led it with de Borre's elevation to division command) wrote, "I marched in front of Gen'l Sullivan's division, when I received orders from him to wheel to the left and take possession of a rising ground about 100 yards in our front, to which the enemy were marching rapidly. I wheeled off, but had not reached the ground, before we were attacked on all quarters, which prevented our forming regularly, and by wheeling to the left it doubled our division on the brigade immediately in the rear of the other. Thus we were in confusion and no person to undue us to order, when the enemy pushed on and soon made us all run off."

In making this maneuver, the front brigade ran into the advancing British Brigade of Guards, who fired, and the 2nd Maryland Brigade in their rear began to fire. Confusion ensued among the Americans, an example of how even experienced troops can be panicked and routed.

Stone continues, "Of all the Maryland regiments only two ever had an opportunity to form, Gist's and mine, and as soon as they began to fire, those who were in our rear could not be prevented from firing also. In a few minutes we were attacked in front and flank, and by our people in the rear. Our men ran off in confusion, and were very hard to be rallied. Although my men did not behave so well as I expected, yet I can scarcely blame them when I consider their situation. . . . My horse threw [me] in the time of action, but I did not receive any great injury from it."[8]

In the meantime, General Howe had set his army in motion, and the British and German troops began moving down from Osborne's Hill. As they stepped off, Lieutenant Colonel William Meadows called out words of encouragement to his troops, the 1st Battalion Grenadiers, "Grenadiers, put on your caps; for damned fighting and drinking I'll match you against the world!" With their distinctive tall miter caps, the grenadiers moved forward.[9]

Howe noted that he saw the Americans "filing off a large number of troops to the rear and toward the right wing where he [Sullivan] had his cannon." He was observing the shifting of troops on Birmingham Hill.[10]

German aide Captain Friedrich von Muenchhausen also noted, "We noticed strong movements from the rebel's right wings to their left ones. They formed two lines in good order along their heights; we could see this because there were some barren places here and there on the hills, which they occupied."[11]

As neither side intended to fight on this particular ground, the action took on a life of its own. Thus the action at Birmingham Hill shows how both sides reacted to unfolding combat conditions. There is perhaps no greater test for troops than to enter battle in this situation: unfamiliar terrain, the ground not scouted, and the enemy strength, intentions, and deployment not known.

Moving south from Osborne Hill, the British and Germans encountered obstacles like fences, stone walls, and hills and valleys. Terrain and foliage interrupted lines of sight, and units were often out of contact with their neighbors on one flank or the other. Most importantly, they certainly could not see the Americans forming ahead of them.

According to an account in the records of the 17th Regiment, the Light Infantry were deployed in files four men deep, an arm's length apart. This allowed them to maneuver more effectively in the woods and when facing obstacles. It is one example of the adaptations the British made over the course of the war.[12]

Following the orders of General Sullivan, Stirling's and Stephen's troops shifted to the right to make room for Sullivan's Marylanders. The American line now had, from left to right, the divisions of Sullivan, Stirling, and Stephen, about 3,400 troops.[13]

This excited maneuvering was unfortunate, for the American line never quite settled in and formed properly. While many of these units had fought together as brigades in the past, some had not, and none had ever maneuvered as divisions in an open field facing the enemy.

Some histories state that Sullivan wanted his division to be positioned on the army's right, the traditional place of honor on the battle line. This would have put them beyond General Stephen's division, forcing them to march over a mile to the east with the Americans already deployed and the British advancing. This was simply not practical given the situation, and no eyewitness accounts mention this. Reality demanded that de Borre move the division a few hundred yards to link up with Sterling's left flank. The misconception has been used to help vilify de Borre, as well as explain the American collapse, yet it appears to be false.[14]

Afterward, in a lengthy letter to clear his name, Sullivan explained his decision making:

> The Enemy pressed on with Rapidity & attacked them which threw them into Some kind of Confusion. I had taken post myself in the Centre with the artillery & ordered it to play briskly to Stop the progress of the Enemy & give the Broken Troops time to Rally & form in the Rear of where I was with the artillery. I sent off four Aid De Camps for this purpose & went myself But all was in vain no Sooner did I form one party but that which I had before formed would Run off & Even at times when I though on Horseback and in front of them apprehended no Danger.

THE BATTLE DEVELOPS AT BIRMINGHAM HILL

I then left them to be Rallied if possible by their own officers & my aid De Camp & Repaired to the Hill where our artillery was which by this time began to feel the Effects of the Enemy's fire. This Hill Commanded both the Right & Left of our Line & if carried by the Enemy I knew would Instantly bring on a Total Rout & make a Retreat very Difficult. I therefore Determined to hold it as Long as possible to give Lord Sterlings & General Stephens Divisions which yet Stood frim as much assistance from the artillery as possible & to give Colo Hazens Daytons & Ogdens Regiments which Still Stood firm on our Left the Same advantage & to Cover the Broken Troops of my Division & give them an opportunity to Rally & come to our assistance which Some of them did & others could not by their officers be brought to do any thing but fly; The Enemy Soon began to bend their principal force against the Hill & the fire was Close & heavy for a Long time & Soon became General. Lord Sterling & General Conway with their Aid De Camps were with me on the Hill & Exerted themselves beyond Description to keep up the Troops.

He summed up his defense, writing, "They met us unexpectedly & in order of Battle & Attacked us before we had time to form & upon Ground we had never before Seen under these Disadvantages & against Those unequal numbers we maintained our Ground."[15]

The shuffling of the American troops caused confusion in an already tense moment. General Weedon noted that "In making this Alteration, unfavorable Ground, made it necessary for Woodford to move his Brigade 200 Paces back of the Line. . . . The Enemy came on rapidly, Scott, who was next to Woodford, was removed to bad Ground . . . in some Confusion."[16]

The American deployment, from left to right, included Sullivan's two Maryland Brigades (1,700 men), coming up but not in line. In line was Dayton (1,060 men), then Conway (about 1,000 men), and lastly Scott (about 800 men) and Woodford (about 1,200 men) on the far right.

Between Conway and Scott was a four-gun battery of three-pounders, and between the two Virginia brigades were two three-pounders unlimbered. The guns had a range of about 1,300 yards,

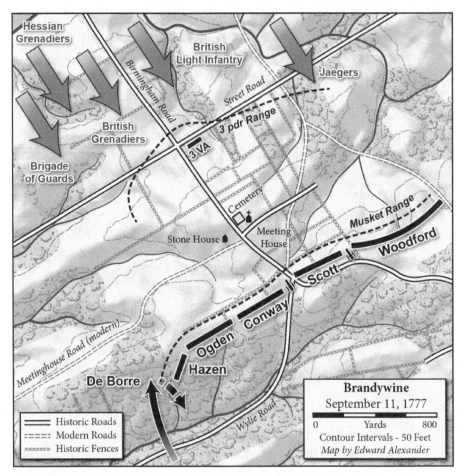

The movement toward Birmingham Hill. The terrain features of this map are based on the USGS Topographic Map, and the historic features such as wood lines, fences, roads, and buildings are based on the Archibald Robertson map in the Royal Collection in London. This map shows the American troop positions at the onset of the action. The size of each American unit is a reflection of its strength. The ranges of their weapons are indicated to show how far artillery was effective, and how close units had to be to engage in musket fire. (*Edward Alexander*)

allowing them to reach as far as Street Road. Due to the rolling terrain and woods they could not pick out distinct targets that far and would have been firing at enemy units as they closed in at closer range.

Top: Conway's Position, looking southeast. Conway's Pennsylvania brigade occupied this high ground in the foreground. In the distance was Dayton's New Jersey brigade, and beyond that is where the Maryland troops were routed. The British advanced from the right. Bottom: Conway's View. Looking north from Conway's position, his troops had this view. The rolling terrain sheltered the advancing British Grenadiers until they emerged over the horizon. They then had to cross the open space to get into musket range. Birmingham Meeting House is to the right front, out of this view. The photos were taken from about the "a" in the word "Conway" on the map opposite this page. (*Author*)

The American troops would have occupied a total of about 1,166 yards (3,500 feet)—nearly two-thirds of a mile—across the crest of Birmingham Hill, based on estimates for the space occupied by nearly 3,500 soldiers. The Maryland units are not included in this calculation, as they were marching up and did not get into position.[17]

The infantry of Sullivan's and Stirling's divisions, armed largely, if not entirely, with muskets, could hit targets effectively about a hundred yards to their front. In most cases this was far closer than they could see, and the Continental troops would have been able to observe the British closing in before they were in range. Modern houses and foliage today obscure much of the view that they had from their line.

In some places, such as in front of Conway's right, the slope gave the approaching British good cover until they were fairly close. Trees and rolling ground also gave the British and Germans protection in front of Stephen's division on the American right.

On the extreme left of the American line was the 2nd Canadian Regiment led by Hazen. Its deployment earlier that morning had kept it separated from the rest of de Borre's brigade. As the senior colonel in the 2nd Maryland Brigade, Hazen likely commanded the brigade with de Borre's ascension to division command. From left to right the brigades of the 1st Maryland, Dayton, Conway, and Scott were in line. Woodford had been forced to pull back to make room for Sullivan's men on the hill.[18]

It was the largest deployment of American troops in an open battle up to that time in the war. For the men in the ranks of Conway's and Scott's brigades who looked to their right and to their left, it must have been an impressive sight, nearly 3,400 troops in formation, supported by artillery.

Across the valley, Generals Howe and Cornwallis observed the Americans forming and shifting their lines. "The damned rebels form well," Cornwallis stated, obviously annoyed at missing the opportunity to gain the hill before the Americans reached it. Regardless, both officers knew their veteran regulars could push the Continentals back, and with their troops rested, orders went out to move the army forward.

Lieutenant General Charles Earl Cornwallis and colonel of the 33rd Regiment of Foot. Cornwallis commanded the division that made the flank march around the American army and attacked at Birmingham Hill. (*Anne S. K. Brown Military Collection, Brown University*)

The elite of the British were going in first: the Brigade of Guards, Grenadiers, Light Infantry, and German Jaegers. Behind them the 3rd Brigade of 1,000 men under General Charles Grey formed on the British right, while General James Agnew's 4th Brigade of 1,400 troops took up the left.[19]

The front line of the British attack included 1,000 troops in the Brigade of Guards, 1,300 men in the Light Infantry Brigade, another 1,400 in the British Grenadier Brigade, and roughly 500 Jaegers on the left flank. Behind the British Grenadiers were about

1,300 in the Hessian Grenadier Brigade. Thus the British and German troops outnumbered and would overlap their adversaries.[20]

Thus began one of the most inspiring spectacles of the entire Revolutionary War: the deployment and advance of nine thousand British and German troops, moving steadily down the slope into the valley, crossing Street Road, and engaging the Americans. The day was clear, and with flags flying and drums beating, it must have impressed all who saw it. For the defenders it would have also been terrifying.

Captain John Montresor, chief engineer for the British army, observed, "Some skirmishing begun in the valley in which the enemy was drove, upon gaining something further of the ascent the enemy began to amuse us with 2 guns." His description matches the movement of the British down from Osborne Hill, across low ground, and up to Birmingham Hill.[21]

Hessian Captain von Muenchhausen wrote,

> At four in the afternoon our two battalions of light infantry and the Hessian jaegers marched down the hill. They marched first in a column, but later, when they approached the enemy, in line formations, deploying to the left. Soon after this the English grenadiers did the same in the center, almost at the same time; just a little later, the English Guards formed the right wing. Behind the English grenadiers were the Hessian grenadiers; behind the light infantry and the jaegers was the 4th English brigade. The 3rd English brigade was in reserve on top of the hill. The two squads of dragoons, who were close to us, halted behind the left wing of the Hessian grenadiers.[22]

The five American cannons on the hill began firing at the British as they advanced into range at Street Road. The British responded by bringing forward six- and twelve-pound guns, most likely into the vicinity of Street Road. Unfortunately there are very few accounts or sources about the artillery of either side. Several of the American guns were brass French pieces and had names inscribed on then like *La Inexorable* and *La Floristante*. Each also had the Latin words *Ultima Ratio Rogum*, meaning "The final argument of kings" engraved on the muzzles.[23]

British Light Infantry, wearing their small leather caps, advance to engage the Americans. General Howe used his best troops: the Light Infantry and Grenadiers, to lead the attack. (*National Park Service*)

At about 3:30 the British stepped off. The men of the 3rd Virginia were making an impact as the British began their advance. A British officer reported that his men "received the fire from about 200 men in an orchard." Their stubborn defense slowed the British advance.[24]

Virginia officer Robert Lawson recalled,

> In the battle of Brandywine he rendered a Service of the utmost importance. The enemy having crossed the river and turned the right of our Army, two divisions were ordered by general Washington to oppose them who marched to take suitable ground for the purpose near Birmingham meeting house—in that occasion general Lawson was ordered by the commanding officer to take post with his Regiment at the meeting house and check the enemy while those divisions were forming. He executed that order to the satisfaction of everyone. He took the position with alacrity, com-

menced a fire on the front of a large column of the enemy, whose march he arrested for some time, the good office whereof was fell by those divisions informing. He then returned with his Regiment in good order and took his Station in the brigade to which he belonged.[25]

According to General George Weedon, Marshall's Virginians "received the Enemy with a Firmness which will do Honor to him and his little Corps, as long as the 11th of Sepr. is remembered. He continued there 3/4 of one Hour, & must have done amazing execution." Whether the Virginians used the tree cover and fought as skirmishers or were line of battle is not known.[26]

As the British moved down from Osborne Hill toward Street Road, Woodford deployed on the American right, about a hundred yards southwest of the stone meeting house. Woodford ordered his 3rd Virginia Regiment forward to the road to stall the British advance. Under the command of Colonel Thomas Marshall, the 170 men of the 3rd Virginia formed up in an orchard on the Jones Farm and began trading fire with the 1st Battalion of Light Infantry to their north, across Street Road. [27]

General Weedon noted that Marshall, "had orders to hold the wood as long as it was tenable & then retreat to the right of the brigade." The Virginians were isolated and in front of the main American line that was forming half a mile behind them on high ground.[28]

The undersized 3rd Virginia moved down the slope to their advanced position close to Street Road. With only 170 present, here in an orchard they suffered greatly in both officers and men. Private Samuel Stribling recalled that they were "nearly all cut off" before pulling back. Charles Lander noted that Captain Cooper was killed and it was a "hard fought battle."[29]

Nineteen-year-old Jeremiah Kendall was wounded in the thigh, which bled profusely. He made it to a nearby house where he was nursed by residents. Phillip Conner, a twenty-five-year-old soldier in the 3rd Regiment, was wounded by a ball through the wrist. Nearby, Private James Arrowsmith was hit in the right ankle.[30]

One of the largest field guns available at the time of the Revolution, a six pound gun fired a solid iron ball of that weight, or exploding shells. Its maximum range was about 1200 yards. The British had several six pound guns at Brandywine to support their advance. (*Author*)

Other losses in the 3rd included Drummer Robert Wharton, who was wounded. At thirty-seven years old, John Neely was one of the older soldiers in the regiment and was bayoneted in the left thigh.[31]

Brothers Charles and James Ailstock of Louisa County were some of the handful of free blacks serving with the 3rd. Both made it through the engagement unscathed.[32]

John Perry, a twenty-nine-year-old private from Charles City County, was not so lucky, being wounded in four places but lived to tell about it. John Oliver was wounded in the thigh.[33]

David Wickliff, a twenty-three-year-old soldier from Prince William County was "severely wounded" but made it out of the collapsing position and survived. Twenty-three-year-old John Matthews of Prince William County recalled that they were "in the hottest" of the action that afternoon. He also recalled the British "marching to within seventy or eighty yards before a gun was fired." Wounded in both legs by a musket ball, he noted, "This Battle was a sore trial to so many parts of the Army."[34]

Losses among the 3rd Virginia's officers were particularly heavy. Sergeant Joshua Jenkins was killed, and Major Peter Moore was wounded when a ball entered his chest, breaking several ribs and passing out his back, two inches to the left of his spine.[35]

The Light Infantry of the 17th and 42nd Regiments advanced against the 3rd Virginia in the Jones orchard. After a brief stand, the Virginians fell back a thousand feet uphill to the shelter of the sturdy stone wall surrounding the Birmingham meetinghouse cemetery. As was customary, Quaker cemeteries did not have headstones, and the Virginians sprawled behind perhaps the best cover enjoyed by any unit on the entire battlefield that day.

A British officer with the 17th Light Infantry Company recalled the "churchyard being opposite the 17th Company. . . . the Captain determined to get over the fence into the road." Captain William Scott yelled at his men to "run down the road," and as they did the "hedge on the left side of the road much cut up with grape shot."

They were then joined by the 38th's company "at the base of the hill," leading up to the crest where the American artillery was firing from. Soon after the 33rd's company arrived. Together they charged up toward the battery and Conway's troops at the crest of the ridge.[36]

The troops of the 17th Light Infantry Company gravitated to a hedge for cover along the west side of the Birmingham Road. Running parallel to the road, it allowed them to gradually work their way past the left flank of the 3rd Virginia at the cemetery wall.

Lt. Frederick Augustus Wetherall of the 17th's Light Infantry Company was in the advance and noted "a High Stone Wall prevented their keeping up with the Battalion, whose companies leap'd over the Fence into the high Road which divided them from the British Grenadiers & in order the sooner to avoid the danger of the Shot ran down the Road & shelter'd themselves at the foot of the Hill." He also noted that the hedge was "much cut with the grape

The 3rd Virginia fell back from the orchard to the cover of this stone wall at the Birmingham Meeting House graveyard. It offered good cover for the Virginians, and they defended this position from the left hand side as the British advanced from the right. Eventually they were outflanked on their left by the British Light Infantry, who advanced into the wooded area in the background. (*Author*)

shot" from the American artillery ahead of them. While not much was going right for the Continental troops, their artillery was effective and numerous British and German accounts note its destruction.[37]

Eventually the British passed by the 3rd Virginia at the stone wall and the Americans' position became untenable. Those Virginians on the left of the line would have noted the enemy's movement. They fell back to their parent unit at the crest of the hill, about two thousand yards behind them. This would have required a heart-pounding dash across open ground, through the heart of the battlefield, with the British Light Infantry close upon them. Colonel Thomas Marshall noted that in the time they were deployed forward they "expended thirty rounds a man, in forty-five minutes." He also noted that "thirteen non-commissioned officers and sixty privates fell."[38]

Colonel Marshall, directing the withdrawal, had two horses shot from under him. Only two captains in the regiment made it out unhurt. Captain John Chilton was killed outright, and Captain Phillip Richard Francis Lee was mortally wounded. In addition, two lieutenants were killed, and thirteen noncommissioned officers and 60 men lost, out of 170. Private Daniel McCarty and his brother carried off Chilton's body.[39]

Captain William Scott of the 17th Regiment's Light Infantry Company noted that they "received a fire from about 200 men in the orchard, which did no execution." He himself may not have felt the Virginians' fire was ineffective, but it certainly delayed the British and caused some casualties.[40]

As the 3rd Virginia was making its stand, confusion and panic soon erupted among the arriving Continental troops on the left flank under de Borre. The 1st Maryland Brigade was just moving into position and not even settled when they came under fire. De Borre's Marylanders never reached their intended position in line, coming under fire as they were approaching behind the 1st Maryland Brigade. As they broke, disorder spread to the troops on their left. Panic is a dangerously contagious thing in linear warfare, and once troops become disrupted in the face of the enemy it is often impossible to contain it. While the Americans and British exchanged some fire at this first position, the confidence and speed of the British attack soon pushed the Americans back.[41]

Sullivan wrote of the arrival of his division at their intended position: "while my division was marching on, and before it was possible for them to form to advantage, the enemy pressed on and attacked them, which threw them into some kind of confusion." He also added, "They were attacked & Thrown into Confusion from which they never fully Recovered."[42]

Colonel John Stone noted that, as the 1st Maryland Regiment was coming up, the British "had begun to cannonade the ground allotted for us, which was very bad, and the enemy within musket shot of it, before we were ordered to form the line of battle." Nothing is known about the order of the regiments marching up in column.[43]

The 1st Maryland Regiment suddenly came face to face with the British Guards, who fired a volley into them. Private George Osborn of the Guards wrote, "We attacked the left flank of the rebel army, and raining upon the brigades of Sullivan . . . with an impetuosity really that it would have been scarcely possible for them to resist . . . we saved much loss we might otherwise have sustained, and certainly made the enemy give way first."[44]

The Maryland troops were some of the Continental Army's best, yet here they were unable to properly maneuver out of a difficult situation. They collapsed and never fought as organized units the remainder of the day. Not only had they not trained on this scale, they had only been engaged in a battle this large once before, at Long Island.

Sullivan saw the collapse from a distance and sent four aides to rally the men, but they "could not be brought by their officers to do any thing but fly." Riding over himself, Sullivan noted, "No sooner did I form one party, but that which I had before formed ran off, and even at times when I though on horseback and in front of them, apprehended no danger. I then left them to be rallied by their own officers."[45]

Sullivan wrote that, "after my own division was broke by being attacked before they were formed." He went on to "attach myself and take command of every other corps that would stand by me."

Sullivan likely was back and forth, coordinating with the various brigade and regimental commanders on the crest.[46]

The Guards attacking the line here sustained few casualties— only one killed, five wounded, and one missing, suggesting that they did not receive much enemy fire here and faced little resistance afterward. The 1st Maryland Regiment lost twenty-six men in the narrow lane, and Colonel John Stone was wounded.

Lieutenant Colonel Samuel Smith of the 4th Maryland Regiment (in the 2nd Brigade) noted that they were marching

> through a narrow lane. The First Brigade of it counter-marched through a gateway, to the top of a hill, under a galling fire from the enemy- thus bringing their rear to their front. Pressed by the enemy, they had no time to form, and gave way at all points. The Second Brigade was formed in a valley in its rear. It was said a retreat had been ordered; but Colonel Smith not knowing it, found himself, to his surprise- being on the left of the Regiment- with only Lieutenant Cromwell and about thirty men. Seeing no enemy, he retired deliberately. Colonel Hazen's Regiment retreated in perfect order.[47]

Smith's ordeal was not over, and he continued his dangerous odyssey: "In passing through a corn-field, Colonel Smith discovered a flanking party of the enemy, which he checked by two fires from his small number and received one from them, by which he lost one man, who was shot in the heel. Some of the men left him; and he retired, almost alone, to the top of a high hill, on which he halted, and collected nearly one thousand men; formed them into Companies; and remained until near sunset."[48]

Captain Enoch Anderson of the Delaware Regiment (part of the 1st Maryland Brigade), wrote that he was in the "center of our Regiment, when Lord Stirling rode up. 'Officer,' says he, 'General Washington is in the rear. Face about!' I did so, as the British were firing on us. I looked about for my Lord [Stirling] to obey his commands, but saw his Lordship whipping and spurring down the road at full gallop! Some of our soldiers were wounded. I thought, 'well, I have no business here fighting in this place . . . the British aimed

A Baltimore merchant before the war, Samuel Smith served in the Philadelphia Campaign with troops from Maryland. After the war he was a delegate in the Maryland legislature, and led federal troops in the Whiskey Rebellion. (*Library of Congress*)

to surround [us] ... and with a quick marching, I [fled with the] ... rest of the Regiment."[49]

Captain Anderson also noted, "Cannon balls flew thick and many from both sides and small arms roared like the rolling of a drum for a considerable time." It was too much for them to stand.[50]

The only unit not caught up in the unfolding disaster was the 2nd Canadian under Hazen, who Sullivan had sent ahead of the rest of his troops. They managed to avoid the confusion of the Marylanders and took up a position, deploying to fight on the hill. From this vantage point they could see to the north and west. As the British closed in on them, they could see the juggernaut coming, and it must have been an uneasy feeling.[51]

General de Borre, acting in command of the division, recalled that "Sullivan's corps' had scarcely had time to form one line in front of a thinly wooded forest." Of course, de Borre himself was caught up in the retreat and did little to stop it.[52]

As the 1st Maryland Brigade unraveled, the 2nd Maryland Brigade came up behind them and got caught up in the withdrawal, many thinking a retreat had been ordered. These troops at the back of the column were below the crest of the hill and had no idea what was unfolding ahead of them. Within minutes they would hear the gunfire ahead and see the frightened troops of the 1st Brigade streaming back, into, and through them, spreading more disorder. Lieutenant Colonel Samuel Smith and Lieutenant Thomas Cromwell tried to restore order, but their efforts were useless in the face of such widespread confusion.[53]

Private John Boudy of the 2nd Maryland Regiment noted that he "received a wound from a musket ball in his knee, which disqualified him from duty in the line till the Winter following." Part of the 2nd Maryland Brigade, these troops in the rear and below the crest of the hill, could likely not see what was unfolding ahead.[54]

Lieutenant William Beatty of the 2nd Maryland Regiment remembered that, as they were maneuvering, "before this could be fully [executed] . . . the Enemy Appeared and made a very Brisk Attack which put the whole of our Right Wing to flight . . . this was not done without some Considerable loss on their side, as of the Right wing behaved Gallantly . . . the Attack was made on the Right, the British . . . made the fire . . . on all Quarter." Sergeant Christopher Parriott was wounded but able to make his way out of the collapsing situation.[55]

Private Jacob Allen, a shoemaker with the 6th Maryland, was "wounded in the hand and in the face" during the brief, confusing encounter. He also noted that his shoulder was dislocated by the fall of branches during the action. Also in the 6th Regiment, fifteen-year-old Michael Palmer was bayonetted in the right groin.[56]

William Leard of the 7th Maryland was wounded in the chest and upper lip but made his way off and survived. Also caught up with the 7th's retreat was Boston Medlar, a seventeen-year-old drummer. Marylander Isaac Whiting suffered a thigh broken by a musket ball.[57]

Henry Wells of the Delaware Regiment remembered that "During the fight, the wind favored the enemy and drove the Smoke directly in our faces which was one great cause of our discomfiture." He was wounded on the right hip and bore the scar the rest of his life.[58]

As Smith was rallying some of the troops, de Borre arrived, and Smith offered him to lead the fragments he collected. Smith noted that de Borre "declined the offer," pointing out wounds to his face. Smith continued to gather the disorganized troops and reform them in the rear, yet they played no further role in the battle.[59]

De Borre was roundly criticized afterward for not only the botched movement to the hill but for his inability to lead the troops and rally them afterward. He claimed in a letter to the Continental Congress, "I done my Duty to go and fetch them to bring again against the enemy. It is not my fault if the americanes troops run away to first fire of enemy . . . [N]obody of them is killed or wounded. I alone received a light wound in the cheek by a bal." He continues, "I didn't know your Language in my arrival in this country, I believed prudently I must Learn it . . . know enough your Language to Wield my orders & to understand that I read."

De Borre resigned two days after the battle. Then later he wrote to Congress on the seventeenth, his sixtieth birthday, to attempt to clear his name. Congress was happy to pay his way back to France.

Sullivan wrote to President of Congress John Hancock, "I never yet have pretend that my Disposition in the Late Battle was perfect, I know it was very far from it but this I will venture to affirm . . . it was the best that time would allow me to make."[60]

General Thomas Conway, commanding the Pennsylvania troops near Birmingham Road, noted, "[i]f part of the Division was not formed completely before the Engagement, The fault can not be imputed to Genl Sullivan, who although he had a right to take the right of the Line, took the Left, in Order to save time, a proof that the Davison of the Right, had full time to form . . ."

He also observed that the "short time left to his troops in order to Form, was hardly sufficient, for well disciplined troops, and well exercised, and by no means sufficient for the troops of this Army, who appear to me to maneauver upon false Principles, and where I cannot discover as yet, The least notion of displaying Columns, and forming briskly upon all Emergencies."[61]

William Wilcox, an aide to General Stirling, wrote that the "enemy by good luck, or perhaps policy, made their attack before the intended disposition of our division . . . could be carried into execution. It was therefore rather to be considered unfortunate, as ill-judged, and not to be laid at the door of any particular officer."[62]

With the Marylanders falling back in disorder, the American deployment consisted, from left to right, of Hazen's unit, the New Jersey regiments under Dayton, Conway's brigade, and Stephen's division on the right.[63]

Sullivan explained that, "I had taken my post in the center" of the American line, possibly with Conway's brigade (which would be about the center), to observe and direct the action and direct the entire force. He also ordered the battery there "to play briskly to stop the progress of the enemy and to give the broken troops time to rally and form in the rear."[64]

Sullivan wrote, "The enemy soon began to bend our principal force against the hill." The firing was "close and heavy for a long time." The brown-coated troops of the 2nd Canadian Regiment under Colonel Hazen held the extreme American left on the hill, facing the German Grenadiers. By now the American units were intermingled and command was beginning to break down. Dayton's Brigade, supported by the 2nd Canadian, held the left, Woodford and Conway the center.[65]

Sergeant Major John H. Hawkins of the 2nd Canadian Regiment recalled, "The weather was very warm, and tho' my knapsack was very light, was very cumbersome, as it swung about when walking or running, and in crossing fences was in the way so I cast it away from me, and had I not done so would have been grabbed by one of the Ill- looking Highlanders, a number of whom were firing and advancing very briskly towards our rear. The smoke was so very thick that about the close of the day I lost sight of our regiment." The fumbling sergeant major lost not only his regiment but his knapsack as well, with all of its contents.

Hawkins also noted that the unit lost four officers and seventy-three men, including Captain Nathan McConnell, who was wounded and later captured, for a total of seventy-seven out of about four hundred, losses of nearly one-quarter. In their exposed position on the end of the American line, they were tempting targets for the advancing British.[66]

While the Maryland troops were collapsing and Hazen was holding out on the American left, the two brigades of Stirling (Dayton and Conway) stood firm to their right. Here the Americans held their ground stubbornly; this would be the most contested part of the field. Both sides traded volleys for several minutes. It was about four o'clock.

The New Jersey Brigade occupied the high ground in the distance, where along with the Canadian Regiment, they bore the brunt of the attack of the British Brigade of Guards from the right and the distant woods at center. The Americans gradually fell back to the left. (*Author*)

Chapter 4

HEART OF
THE BATTLE

"A most infernal fire."
—Lieutenant Richard St. George, 52nd Light Infantry

THE NEW JERSEY REGIMENTS, and Hazen's Canadians with them, were deployed on the highest ground on Birmingham Hill. From their position they could see the British advancing from the north and northwest. To the right of Dayton's New Jersey brigade were Conway's Pennsylvanians, and this chapter will explore the action on their part of the line before moving on to the Virginians on the far right.

Advancing steadily toward these troops were the British Brigade of Guards and Grenadiers. As the battle unfolded, casualties mounted, muskets became too hot to hold, weapons fouled, and smoke obscured movement. As British fire hit its mark, the New Jersey and Pennsylvania soldiers found themselves stepping over their dead and wounded comrades as they loaded and fired. This intense combat, in the open, with the enemy closing in, was unlike anything these soldiers had experienced before.

Colonel Elias Dayton of the 3rd New Jersey wrote of his command that,

> between 3 and 4 o'clock in the afternoon, [we] formed the largest part of the three divisions upon a hill near Birmingham meeting house. The enemy very soon advanced to attack, I believed before Gen. Sullivan's division was formed, as they changed their ground on which they drew up. A number of them were marching past my regiment when the fire first began, consequently I believe we never fired a gun. In half an hour at farthest, the whole of our men gave way; the enemy pursued briskly, by which means a number of our wounded, as also some well men fell into their hands, in the whole about four hundred, and six or eight pieces of brass cannon six pounders.[1]

Major Joseph Bloomfield, also of the 3rd, wrote,

> It is well known that after we rallied the first time & broke & were closely pursued by the British-Grenadiers that Capt. Bellard of our Regt. who was wounded in the leg & would have fallen into the hands of the Enemy had I not (though I have the Modesty to say it myself) went back upon his crying for assistance, taken him behind me & brought him from the Field of Battle: & must undoubtedly have been killed had not the Enemys fire been expended & they relyed on their Bayonetts in their pursuit as their front was within a few Yards of us when I rode off with Capt. Bellard.[2]

Bloomfield himself was wounded, "having a Ball with the Wad shot through my Left forearm & the fuse set my coat and shirt on fire." In addition to the incoming British musket fire, he now had to contend with his smoldering coat.[3]

Lieutenant Ebenezer Elmer, surgeon's mate in the 3rd New Jersey, captured the desperation of the fighting in his long-winded account:

> we came in sight of the enemy who had crossed the river & were coming down upon us; we formed abt. 4 o'clock on an Eminence, the right being in the woods, presently a large Column came on us in front playing the Grenadiers March & now the battle began

A seasoned commander, Col. Elias Dayton led the New Jersey Brigade at Brandywine. After the war he served as mayor of Elizabethton and in the state general assembly. (*New York Public Library*)

which Proved excessive severe the Enemy came on with fury our men stood firing upon them most amazingly, killing almost all before them for near an hour till they got within 6 rods [about 100 feet] of each other, when a column of the Enemy came upon our right flank which caused them to give way which soon extended all along the line; we retreated & formed on the first ground and gave them another fire & so continued on all the way, but unfortunately for want of a proper retreat 3 or 4 of our pieces were left on the first ground.[4]

Joseph Clark, a twenty-six-year-old staff officer formerly with the 2nd New Jersey, was on Stephen's staff that day. He wrote, "as their number was larger than was expected, they stretched their line beyond ours and flanked our right wing shortly after the action began." By "right wing" he is referring to all three divisions. Clark then continued, "This caused the line to break, to prevent being surrounded, though the firing while the action lasted was the warmest I believe that has been in America since the War began;

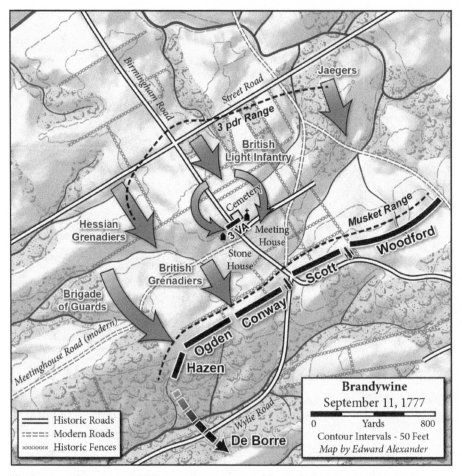

The battle on Birmingham Hill opening movements. The 3rd Virginia has fallen back from the orchard to the stone wall at the Meeting House. The Brigade of Guards and British Grenadiers are engaged with Hazen, Ogden, and Conway, while the Light Infantry and Jaegers are advancing toward Scott and Woodford. (*Edward Alexander*)

and, as our men on the left of the lien were pretty well stationed, they swept off great numbers of the enemy before they retreated." In referring to the left of the line he is speaking of the New Jersey brigade of Dayton.[5]

British artillery deployed above Street Road and began to open fire to assist the infantry advance. The artillery included two twelve-pounders northeast of the Street Road/Birmingham Road intersection and another two twelve-pounders directly to the north, on high ground overlooking Street Road. With a maximum range of about 1,666 yards (4,900 feet), the Americans were well within range.

The British Guards and Grenadiers, advancing uphill from Street Road, faced numerous obstacles. In the valley of Street Road, the slope and woods hid the Americans from the front. The American line was about one third of a mile away, well out of musket range, but as they advanced, the British entered well within the range of the American artillery.

The British Guards moved down from Street Road, through the fencing that Joseph Townsend mentioned tearing down, and then came to a second fence. After negotiating that, they descended into a ravine with a creek and then rose up to the open field where Sullivan's division waited.

Those British on the right had an easier time, for the troops on the left faced a steep slope, but it also hid them from direct artillery fire. The troops to the right, coming up against Dayton, were also more exposed, crossing open ground, whereas the soldiers on the left, approaching Conway, were sheltered but could not see their foes until they ascended the last slope, about 160 yards in front of the Americans. With muskets loaded, the British moved rapidly to close in, hearts pounding and canteens, cartridge boxes, and bayonet scabbards banging and clanging.

There were roughly 1,060 troops of Dayton's New Jersey Brigade, along with Hazen's Canadian Regiment, which clung tenaciously on the flank and added another four hundred muskets. Assuming a rate of firing two volleys a minute, the left-most American unit on Birmingham Hill was firing about two thousand projectiles per minute. Such a rate could not be maintained long, for muskets would foul and flints would crack or become dull. Nor would they want to expend all of their ammunition. The large size of Dayton's and Hazen's units likely enabled them to hold out as long as they did, despite being flanked and facing some of the British army's most elite troops.

For these Americans it was likely unnerving, as they witnessed the collapse of the Marylanders on their left and could see the

British coming at them, yet could not fire till they were within range. They likely caught glimpses of the British emerging and disappearing as they moved through the swales toward them.

British engineer Captain John Montresor described the terrain south of Street Road, "gradually as it were rose, a regular Glacis to the Enemy." A glacis is a slope that leads up to a fortification; clearly Montresor was comparing the Continental position to a fort. He also noted that the men were "sultry and dusty and rather fatigued" by the movement.[6]

As Hazen's Canadian Regiment stood firm, firing, Captain Matthew McConnell's leg was struck and broken, and Private Francis Tiscount was wounded in the left arm. The unit lost seventy-seven of about four hundred engaged, about a fifth of their strength. During the retreat Private John Sweeney was among those taken prisoner.[7]

Private William Deakins of the Canadian Regiment, who with dark brown hair stood five feet, one inch and was often "laughed at by comrades" for his height, was wounded in the left shoulder. Deakins made it off the field during the withdrawal and survived. Drummer Phillip Nagel of the Canadian Regiment recalled seeing Sergeant Nicholas Lott "severely wounded," and reflecting on his unit, he wrote "a Number of Men wounded."[8]

The 2nd New Jersey Regiment lost much more heavily in officers than men: its colonel wounded, a captain and sergeant killed, a corporal wounded, and three soldiers missing and one wounded. Commanding officer Colonel Israel Shreve was wounded in the thigh in the action. Forty-year-old Joseph Stout was the captain killed.[9]

Captain Jonathan Forman of the 4th New Jersey wrote that they fought until "they were Almost at Bayonet Pts. but we were forc.d to Retreat in Disorder, the En.y Closely Pursuing." The troops from New Jersey were under tremendous pressure and were gradually pushed back.[10]

To the right of the New Jersey troops, the brown-coated Pennsylvania soldiers of Conway's brigade had their right resting on the Birmingham Road. The two ranks faced to the north, along the military crest, the part of the slope that allowed them to see the enemy coming, just down from the topographical crest. The plowed field in front of them gave them a clear field of fire across the undulating ground which the British Grenadiers had to cross. Standing in two ranks, firing at the enemy, the soldiers loaded and fired on command, with volleys going downrange toward the British. Yet, in a compact mass, incoming fire often hit and disabled many men at one time.

Upon finally emerging from the swales that gave them cover, the British had to cross three hundred yards of open ground, all exposed to artillery fire, and then enter the Pennsylvanians' musket range when a hundred yards from them. The regular marching pace, the common step, was a two-foot stride, done at eighty steps per minute. Quick time elevated the pace to a hundred steps per minute. At this faster pace, troops could cover about 66 to 80 yards per minute. Some of the Grenadiers had to move around a stone house, and many likely stopped there for shelter. This house still stands on the battlefield.[11]

The position of individual units is not known, so regimental accounts from Conway's brigade are recounted here in numerical order. Pennsylvania soldier Andrew Swallow later wrote that they deployed on a hill, referring to the high ground on which Conway's brigade stood.[12]

Ensign William Russell of the 3rd Pennsylvania lost a leg in the fighting, while Private John Francis, an African-American in the 3rd, had both legs "much shattered by grape shot." Stacey Williams in the 6th Pennsylvania, another Black soldier, was wounded in the right thigh.[13]

Private Adam Koch of the 9th Pennsylvania, a Berks County soldier, was wounded by a musket ball in the face, which "injured his hearing." The ball entered below his right eye and passed out below his right ear. Privates Peter Eager, Joseph McMahon, Benjamin Coats, William Moody, Hugh McIntosh, William Collins, Duncan Keenon, John Scott, Joseph Brown, Francis King, William Redman, Jerry Connel, Joseph Shaw, and William Smith were all wounded, as were Corporal William Fegan and Sergeant Hugh Cull.[14]

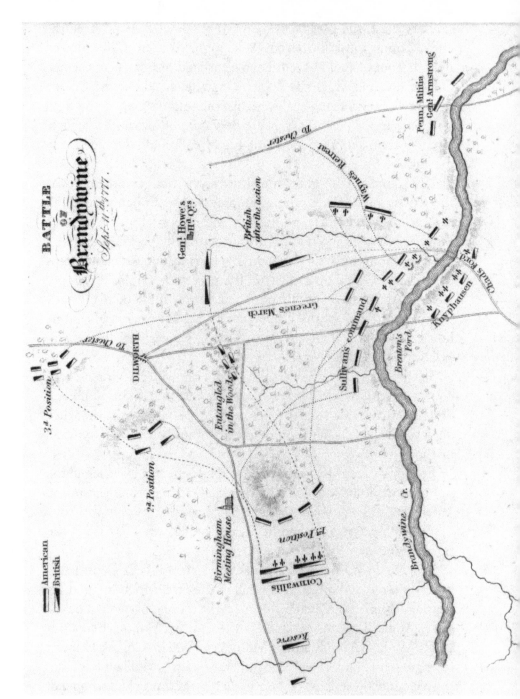

The Battle of Brandywine, September 11, 1777. This nineteenth-century map shows the various positions before, during, and after the battle. (*New York Public Library*)

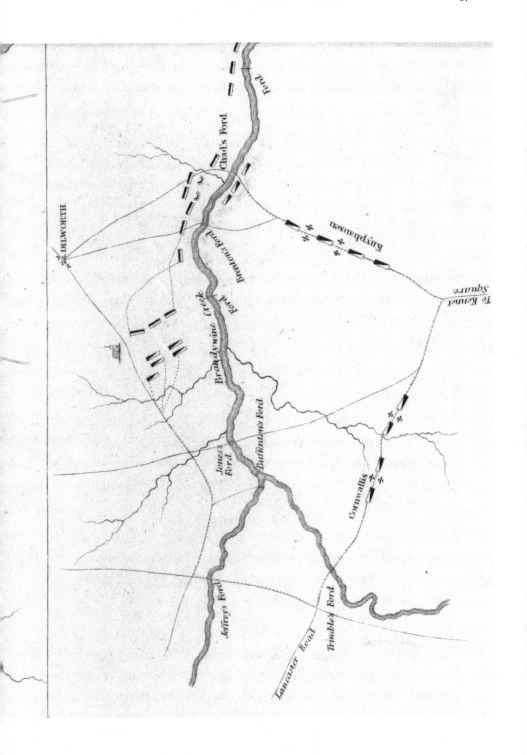

Ensign Benjamin Morris of the 9th and Privates David Mullen, Peter Johnson, James McClellan, John Spence, Peter Miller, Samuel Hall, and Samuel Mullen were killed. Loading and firing out in the open, the men had no cover.[15]

Private Alexander Williamson of the 9th Pennsylvania fell wounded but made his way safely off the field. Private Samuel Collins of the 9th was wounded in the left ankle. He later recalled that he was "taken to a large Brick Meetinghouse that was occupied as a hospital." Collins was taken to the nearby Birmingham Meeting House, which was filled with wounded after the battle.[16]

Captain William Mackey was wounded by a ball through his lungs and was later captured. Overall the 9th Regiment suffered about 40 casualties that afternoon, with 8 killed, 16 wounded, and 16 missing out of about 239 men on the field. Nearly every sixth man in the regiment fell.[17]

An 1845 visitor to the site of this stand, Dr. William Darlington, recorded an eyewitness account. He wrote of walking the ground with then-Captain McClellan, who commanded a company in the 9th Pennsylvania:

> The late Col. McClellan, of this county, who was a captain in the American army, pointed out to me the position which his company occupied on the left wing of the line. . . . It was on the eminence immediately south of the road where it turns at right angles to the east and west, about a quarter of a mile south of the meeting-house. He said when the British approached them, a stout man whom he took to be a Scotchman, and who was evidently under the influence of liquor, advanced recklessly and placed himself behind a little mound, made by the root of a tree which had been blown down. From this position, which was within pistol-shot of McClellan's company, the British soldier fired, and killed the sergeant, who was standing by Capt. McClellan's side. This, of course, attracted McClellan's notice. Capt. McClellan, seeing his sergeant fall, and observing whence the fatal missile came, perceived that the man was reloading his piece as he lay crouched behind the mound, and partially protected by it, and determined to anticipate

A detail from this 1873 map by A. R. Witmer shows the roads and houses at that time. The Birmingham Road runs down the center of the map, with Street Road running left to right. "F.M.H." in the center notes the Birmingham Friends Meeting House. To the left of that, and below it, are marked the Continental battle positions. Note Mrs. Pepper's house just to the south. In the upper left, the starting position of Cornwallis is noted. (A. R. Witmer, *Atlas of Chester County, Pennsylvania*)

him. He discharged his carbine with deliberate aim, and said he saw the soldier roll over, evidently disabled, if not killed.[18]

Darlington also wrote, "The American line . . . on the slightly rising ground some eighty or one hundred rods southeastward of the Birmingham meeting-house. . . . The extreme left of the line was at the spot where stands the rural cottage of Mrs. Pepper, and the company of Capt. Joseph McClellan occupied that position."[19]

On the 1873 Witmer Map of Chester County, the Pepper House is clearly shown, as are troop positions, based on local tradition. This map shows the battle positions in the same location as the 1856 Kennedy Map, overleaf, suggesting a long history of accurate local tradition.[20]

McClellan then stated that they retreated across Bennet's field, south of Wistar's woods, where musket balls were found afterward

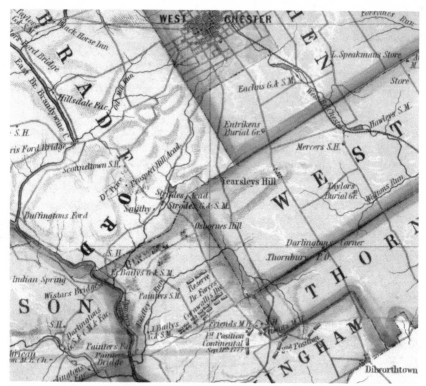

This detail from an 1856 map of Chester County, Pennsylvania, by J. T. Kennedy shows the initial American position on the high ground, toward the bottom of the map, as well as the positions of the British army. Brandywine Creek is to the west. (*Library of Congress*)

for years. McClellan had commanded Company F of the 9th Pennsylvania during the battle.[21]

The 12th Pennsylvania suffered heavily in officers as they stood their ground, with Major James Crawford wounded and Second Lieutenant William Boyd killed. Private Jacob Cook was hit in the right leg. Captain John Brady and his fifteen-year-old son John were also both wounded. Brady commanded Company D from Northumberland County in central Pennsylvania.[22]

Among the troops of Spencer's Additional Regiment (from New Jersey), Andrew Thompson was captured. Unfortunately, their losses in killed and wounded are not known, and few accounts from this unit have surfaced.[23]

With soldiers constantly loading and firing, Conway's Pennsylvanians would have been enshrouded in smoke. Black powder residue stained the soldiers' fingers, and their cheeks were equally stained from tearing open cartridges with their teeth. General Conway wrote that he "never saw so close and severe a fire."[24]

It is not known how long the Americans held this initial position on the crest of Birmingham Hill. Under pressure from the advancing British Grenadiers and Guards, Hazen's, Dayton's, and Conway's troops fell back to the higher ground behind them, below (south of) modern Wylie Road. Here they made another stand, though it is not certain how long or how organized it was, as accounts lack these details.

To Conway's right, deployed between his and Scott's brigades, were four three-pound brass guns. Set up on the crest in or near the Birmingham Road, they provided crucial support to the infantry. The guns had a maximum range of about 1,000 yards. Thus they could hit targets as far down as Street Road, meaning the British were in range for most of their assault. Yet the wooded and broken nature of the ground, along with obstacles like the Birmingham Meeting House and another stone house, prevented a clear view for the gunners. They would have caught glimpses of the redcoats as they moved among the woods and hills.

Artilleryman Elisha Stevens wrote of the British artillery fire, "and the fire took such effect that it would cut a swath right through and sweep down whole companies as it were in an instant, upon which our men could close and fill up the vacancy and in an instant have the same fate."[25]

He also recalled the scene: "Cannons roaring, muskets cracking, Drums Beating Bombs Flying all Round, men a dying & wounded Horred Grones." His words are a good reminder of the confusion, chaos, and terror of eighteenth-century linear combat.[26]

While Hazen and Stirling's men were becoming fully engaged on the left, the action picked up in front of Scott's and Woodford's brigades of Stephen's division. The Hessian Jaegers under von Wurmb were moving ahead on the far British left flank. The Hessian and Anspach Jaegers encountered challenging terrain as they moved over Street Road and toward Stephen's troops. The ground ahead of them was hilly and wooded, obscuring vision and making communication difficult.

Civilian Joseph Townsend saw the Hessian Jaegers engage the Americans as the battle started. He wrote,

> [W]e had a grand view of the army as they advanced over and down the south side of Osborne's Hill. . . . While we were amusing ourselves with the wonderful curiosity before us, to our great astonishment and surprise the firing of the musketry took place; the advanced guard aforementioned having arrived at the street road, and were fired upon by a company of the Americans, who were stationed in the orchard north of Samuel Jones' brick dwelling house. The attack was immediately returned by the Hessians, by their stepping up the bank of the road alongside of the orchard, making the fence as a breast work through which they fired upon the company who made the attack.[27]

Townsend then described the bars, or fences:

> I arrived at the aforementioned bars on the road, which opened into the field of Amos Davis, where I was met by several companies of soldiers, who were ordered into the field to form and prepare for the approaching engagement—the opening of the bars was not of sufficient width to admit them to pass . . . A German officer on horse back ordered the fence to be taken down, and as I was near to the spot, I had to be subject to his requirings as he flourished a drawn sword over my head with the others who stood by; on the removal of the second rail, I was forcibly struck with the impropriety of being active in assisting to take the lives of my fellow beings, and therefore desisted proceeding any further in obedience to his commands.[28]

Captain Johann Ewald, commanding the Hessian Jaegers on the far left of the advance, wrote,

> About half past three I caught sight of some infantry and horsemen behind a village on a hill in the distance. I drew up at once and deployed. . . . I reached the first houses of the village with the flankers

American artillery provided valuable support for the infantry on Birmingham Hill. The Americans had 3 pound guns in action there, like the one firing in demonstration above. (*National Park Service*)

of the jagers, and Lt. Hagen followed me with the horsemen. But unfortunately for us, the time this took favored the enemy and I received extremely heavey small-arms fire from the gardens and houses, through which, however, only two jagers were wounded. Everyone ran back, and I formed them again behind the fences or walls at a distance of two hundred paces from the village.[29]

The village Ewald refers to is likely the few houses and Birmingham Meeting House.

By this time the British 4th, 33rd, and 38th Regiments arrived, reinforcing the 17th Light Infantry Company near Birmingham Road. Captain William Scott of the 17th Light Infantry Company noted that they "caught a glimpse of the enemy as far as they could reach to the right and left." In looking up, they were seeing all of Conway's Pennsylvania brigade deployed on the crest above them.[30]

Scott explained that they were "compelled to throw ourselves on our knees and bellies, and keep up a fire from the slope of the hill."

Augustus Wetherall said that "The Inspiration & Courage of both Officers & Men including them to ascend the Heights, the whole Rebel Line presented itself to View & so close that those who compos'd this spirited Attack had nothing to Expect but Slaughter."[31]

As the main American line, with Dayton's and Conway's brigades, was fully engaged with the British Grenadiers and Light Infantry, the most casualties likely occurred here. Maximum musket range was a hundred yards, so the British moved in a bit closer to make their fire effective. Then, volleying and reloading, both sides blazed away. The results were the casualties noted in the previous paragraphs.

Captain William Scott of the 17th Light Infantry Company noted, "the enemy repeatedly attempted to come on, but were always drove back by our fire. At this time a most tremendous fire of musketry opened from both sides."

Captain William Dansey, who commanded the 33rd Light Infantry Company, was hit in the joint of his right thumb. Writing afterward, he said it could have been worse, as he feared losing his head in the intense musketry. The rest of the Light Infantry companies were pinned behind the fence running out from Birmingham Road, about a hundred yards behind the advanced companies.[32]

The British 1st Grenadier Battalion deployed about forty paces from Dayton's New Jersey troops. A British officer noted the Americans fired "a whole volley and sustained a very heavy fire" on his men, going on to note it was "the heaviest firing I ever heard . . . continuing a long time, every inch of ground being disputed."[33]

British attacks were taking their toll, and soon the 2nd Canadian Regiment and Conway's brigade were wavering. By now a group of French officers (including Lafayette) had arrived and assisted with rallying troops. Lafayette had recently arrived at the army and was serving as an aide without a battlefield command.

Von Metuchen saw bayonet fighting and hand-to-hand combat, something rare in battle during the war. The British Grenadiers "fired a volley, and then ran furiously at the rebels with fixed bayonets." An officer with the British Grenadiers noted, "we had the

LE MARQUIS DE LA FAYETTE
Marechal de Camp.

The Marquis de Lafayette, left, in a contemporary engraving, fought his first battle with the American army at Brandywine. The young French officer rallied troops, right, bravely and calmly directing them in the thick of the fighting. (*New York Public Library; Library of Congress*)

most dreadful fire for one hour I ever saw. I heard nothing equal to it all last war in Germany. At last we gave the rebels the bayonet, which soon dispersed them."[34]

Chevalier Dubuysson, an aide with Lafayette, wrote about joining Conway's brigade: "The Marquis de Lafayette joined the latter, where there were some Frenchmen. He dismounted and did his utmost to make the men charge with fixed bayonets." At one point he even "pushed them in the back to make them charge." Dubuysson noted that the "Americans are not suited for this type of combat, and never wanted to take it up."[35]

Lafayette, endeavoring to rally the troops and lead counterattacks, wrote that eventually order broke down among the Pennsylvanians, writing that "confusion became extreme." The twenty-year old Frenchman tried to prevent them from breaking when a ball "passed through his leg." Then "the remaining forces gave way, and [he] was fortunate to be able to mount a horse, thanks to Gimat [his aide]. . ." At the same time, another French officer, Captain Francois Louis de Fleury, had his horse shot from under him. With no other choice, Lafayette then joined in the withdrawal to the southeast. Colonel Heman Swift of Washington's staff was on hand and used his sash to wrap Lafayette's wound. It was the start of a lifetime friendship.[36]

Lieutenant Henry Stirke of the 10th Light Infantry Company, fighting to the east against Stirling's right (Conway's brigade), noted, "under a heavy fire both of Cannon and small arms, notwithstanding which, and the difficulty of the ground we had to march over, we push'd the Rebels from ye heights, in about 15 minutes, with great loss." His estimate of the time seems too short when compared to other accounts.[37]

General Howe wrote that his troops were "under a heavy train of artillery and musquetry; but they pushed on with an impetuosity not to be sustained by the enemy." The general remained at the rear, either on Osborne Hill or perhaps as close as Street Road, to direct the operation.[38]

Captain John Montresor reported, "The British Grenadiers and Guards at the same time laboring under a smart and incessant fire from the Rebels out of a wood and above them, most nobly charged them without firing a shot and drove them before them." His account captures the general movement but glosses over the resistance that the defenders put up.[39]

Sir George Osborn commanded the Guards Light Company and Guards Grenadier Company on the right flank of the British advance. He noted that "we attacked the left flank of the rebel army. . . . I had but one Grenadier wounded, the Light Company who were with me had only three."[40]

General Sullivan observed, "The enemy soon began to bend their principal force against the Hill, & the fire was close & heavy for a Long time & soon became General . . . five times did the Enemy drive our Troops from the Hill & as often was it Regained & the Summit often Disputed almost muzzle to muzzle. . . . The General fire of the Line Lasted an hour & forty minutes Fifty one minutes of which the Hill was disputed almost Muzzle to Muzzle in such a manner that General Conway who has seen much Service Says he never Saw so close & Severe a fire—on the Right where General Stephen was it was Long & Severe & on the Left Considerable." Sullivan's statement about five charges is probably an exaggeration, but it speaks to the intensity of the fighting.[41]

As they pushed the Pennsylvanians back, Captain William Scott of the 17th Light Infantry Company noted that he "saw Captain Cochrane of the 4th company on my left throw up his cap and cry 'Victory!' and, looking round, saw the 43rd company hastening to our relief." They "dashed forward, passed the five pieces of cannon which the enemy had abandoned, and made some few prisoners, the enemy running away from us, with too much speed to be overtaken."[42]

Surgeon Richard Howell with the 2nd New Jersey Regiment noted, "We had been there but a short time when they appeared, and the heaviest fighting I ever heard began, continuing, every inch of ground being disputed." He noted that "Colonel Shreve . . . was wounded in that action, but not mortally," and Captain Strout was killed. He continued, "After having been among them, with the loss of my mare, saddle and bridle, and great coat and hat, with all my misfortunes I think myself happy, not to be taken prisoner."[43]

Sullivan recalled that, "When we found the right and left oppressed by numbers and giving way on all quarters, we were obliged to abandon the hill we had so long contended for, but not till we had almost covered the ground between that and Birmingham meetinghouse with the dead bodies of the enemy." Again, this is an exaggeration by Sullivan after the fact when defending his reputation.

Author Michael Harris explained that, starting in 1776, the British troops had been instructed to drop to the ground as the Americans prepared to fire, thus reducing casualties and possibly giving the false impression of taking losses. This was part of their adjustment to fighting in North America.[44]

Sullivan later claimed that his troops (those of Stirling and Stephen) repulsed five charges on the hill and held out for an hour and forty-five minutes. Of course, this depends on what is defined as a charge, and the estimate of time is hard to judge. British accounts do note that Conway's Pennsylvanians did advance, at least a little, but whether they were charges, or countercharges, is difficult to say.[45]

The British Grenadier Battalion lost 24 killed and 126 wounded, testifying to the greater intensity of combat against the New Jersey and Pennsylvania troops than the Guards faced versus the quickly routed Marylanders. These were significant losses to some of the elite troops of Howe's army, and the reduced numbers in the Grenadier Battalion would be felt later at the Battle of Germantown.

Captain George Harris of the 5th Grenadier Company saw Lieutenant Colonel William Meadows, commander of the 1st Grenadier Battalion, go down wounded. Harris wrote, "He received a shot, in the act of waving his sword-arm just above the elbow, that went out at the back, knocking him off his horse, and the fall breaking his opposite collar-bone." Meadows had encouraged his men at the start of the action, calling on their reputation as fighters and drinkers.[46]

As might be expected, there was rivalry between the German and British troops. Lieutenant William Hale of the 2nd Battalion of British Grenadiers wrote of the Germans, "I believe them steady, but their slowness is of the greatest disadvantage in a country almost covered with wood." He noted that the Hessian Grenadiers behind them "began their march at the same time as us." But "from that minute we saw them no more till the action was over, and only one man of them was wounded." From their light losses and few accounts, it seems the German Grenadiers fell behind and did not keep up with the advance.[47]

A member of the Minnigerode Grenadier Battalion of the Hessian Grenadiers recalled that "We moved forward, passing through a forest. When we reached a height the Guards, which were on the right wing, continued through ... and vanished." Clearly even professional troops like the British and German forces here could have problems deploying and maneuvering over unknown ground, broken by hills, ravines, and woods.[48]

Although not heavily engaged, the Hessian Grenadiers did suffer casualties. A report noted that "Of the von Linsing Battalion, Lieutenants Dupuy and von Baumbach were slightly wounded, and some noncommissioned officers besides, the von Lengerke Battalion lost a fine grenadier, who was suffocated during the attack on account of the rapid march and the great heat."[49]

Eventually Conway's and Dayton's troops were pushed back from their second position on the higher ground and fell back in disorder through the wooded low ground behind them. Rushing over the American dead and wounded the British Brigade of Guards and Grenadiers kept the pressure on the Continental troops, and they soon broke from this position.

During the retreat, Irish-born Captain Thomas Butler of the 3rd Pennsylvania rallied and encouraged his men as they fell back. His four brothers, William, Percival, Richard and Edward, also served in the war. Washington personally thanked Captain Butler for his leadership that day.[50]

To the right, or east, of Conway's brigade stood the Virginians of Woodford's and Scott's brigades. These troops defended high ground just to the north of a local landmark known as Sandy Hollow.

Soldiers in the British army endured strict discipline, but their morale was high and they were motivated to achieve their objectives. (*National Park Service*)

Chapter 5

THE FIGHT FOR SANDY HOLLOW

"Nothing to expect but slaughter."
—Captain William Scott, 17th Light Infantry

WHILE DAYTON AND CONWAY ENGAGED the British Guards and Light Infantry on the American left, the right of the line was held by two Virginia brigades of Woodford and Scott. The action here unfolded at the same time as the events on the American left.

With Woodford's brigade on the right, and Scott's brigade on the left, next to Conway's, Stephen's Division faced British Light Infantry and German Jaegers. The Americans were on high ground that was an extension of Birmingham Hill. To their south, the land sloped down to Sandy Hollow. The 1st Light Infantry Battalion advanced along Birmingham Road, past the site of the 3rd Virginia's initial stand, and engaged Scott's five Virginia regiments. The 2nd Light Infantry Battalion and Hessian and Anspach Jaegers moved forward to come to grips with Woodford's regiments. Agnew's 4th Brigade came up behind these advanced troops to support the Light Infantry.

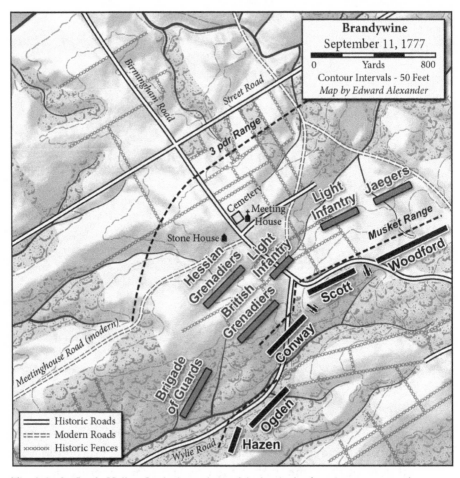

The fight for Sandy Hollow. In the later phase of the battle the American troops on the left have been pushed back and are making a stand on higher ground, while the Light Infantry and Jaegers assault Scott and Woodford. (*Edward Alexander*)

Lieutenant Colonel Ludwig von Wurmb, commander of the German Jaegers, wrote, "I saw that the enemy wanted to form for us on a bare hill, so I had them greeted by our two amusettes." Amusettes were large guns, mounted on poles, which could provide extra support for the advancing Jaegers.[1]

Staff officer Captain von Muenchhausen of Hanover wrote, "As soon as the third column had formed, the signal to march was drummed everywhere. When we got close to the rebels, they fired their cannons; they did not fire their small arms till we were within 40 paces of them, at which time they fired whole volleys and sustained a very heavy fire. The British, and especially the grenadiers, advanced fearlessly and very quickly; fired a volley, and then ran furiously at the rebels with fixed bayonets."[2]

A German officer noted that Stephen's troops were "advantageously posted on a not especially steep height in front of a woods, with the right wing resting on a steep and deep ravine." Stephen's regiments enjoyed the advantage of an open field of fire to their front. The two guns of Stephen's division were quite effective, inflicting casualties on their attackers, forcing them to seek cover, and no doubt providing a morale boost to their nearby infantry.[3]

Lieutenant Richard St. George of the 52nd's Light Infantry Company described "a most infernal Fire of cannon & musketry—most incessant shouting—incline to the right! Incline to the Left!—halt!—charge! . . . the balls ploughing up the ground. The Trees cracking over ones head, The branches riven by the artillery—The leaves falling as in autumn by grapeshot." During the action St. George was hit: "A ball glanced against my ancle & contused it."[4]

In the same company, twenty-year-old Lieutenant Martin Hunter saw that "The position the enemy had taken was very strong indeed—very commanding ground, a wood on their rear and flanks, a ravine and strong paling in front. The fields in America are fenced in by paling."[5]

Woodford's brigade, consisting of the 3rd, 7th, 11th, and 15th Virginia, anchored the American far right. As with the other brigades, it is not known where individual regiments were deployed. The 7th Virginia had over 470 men in the fight, and most wore dark hunting frocks in contrast to military-style coats.

Like the 3rd Regiment, the 7th lost heavily in officers. Captain Reuben Lipscomb from King William County had only been in command a short time and was killed. Several accounts and remembrances from men in the 7th Regiment have survived.[6]

Jesse Sanders, a twenty-three-year-old private, was a few steps away when Colonel Alexander McClanahan's horse was shot from under him. Escaping injury during that incident, Sanders then caught Captain Matthew Jouett who fell wounded, wrapping his arms around the officer and helping him to the ground.[7]

Private James Mason of the 7th Virginia was wounded in the left leg and had his big toe shot off. While falling back, he passed over the body of Lieutenant Levi Grooms, who had been hit and killed. Comrades described Grooms as an "amiable and promising young man." Leonard Shackleford saw Sergeant Noah Taylor wounded.[8]

Sergeant Banks Dudley of the 7th Virginia had a musket ball enter one side of his mouth and pass out the other, taking off all of his upper teeth. Years later it was recorded that "a Ball has passed thro' the upper Jaws, that all the neighbouring Bones have been greatly Injured; that the wound is still open, & its hole so exceedingly large as now to require a Tent of three or four Inches in Length & more than an inch in diameter, that without this Tent worn Constantly he can neither Speak or Swallow but with the utmost difficulty; that a very offensive & considerable discharge is still kept up from the wound – his sufferings have been extremely great." Among the soldiers wounded were Private James Davenport and Simon Green.[9]

Francis Boyd was wounded and captured. He noted that a "ball has passed through the Joint of the Left knee and greatly diminished . . . thereof." Twenty-nine-year-old James Curtis was shot through both legs, the left being quite severely injured.[10]

John Malone, a twenty-six-year-old soldier from Hampton, was wounded, lost sight in his right eye, and was captured. Joseph Bybee of Fluvanna County was wounded in the leg, never able to walk properly again.[11]

Private Royal Lockett recalled later that he saw Lafayette wounded among the Pennsylvania troops to the west. Lockett must have been looking that way at the right moment to see the incident on the other side of Birmingham Road.[12]

There were over 370 men in the 11th Virginia, and its ranks had many riflemen. Irish-born Captain James Calderwood of the 11th Virginia was killed, and Lieutenant Thomas Lucas took his place in command.[13]

Privates Robert Mitchell and Joseph Garner were wounded in the left arm. John Casey, twenty-eight years old, was struck in two places in the left arm, resulting in a broken bone. Isaac Brown was wounded in the leg.[14]

Eighteenth-century combat was brutal and random in its violence. Private Nicholas White was wounded twice and "suffered much pain and inconvenience" as a result. Nearby, Peter Bryan was hit by a spent ball but was not seriously injured, and three of the Potts brothers from Loudon County fought side by side, all surviving: John, Jonathan, and David.[15]

Many in the 11th Virginia suffered painful and debilitating injuries. William Broughton was bayonetted through the fleshy part of his arm and into his throat. Private John Alverson was wounded in the left hand, with two fingers shot off, and was also stabbed in the right thigh and leg. Chaplain John Cordell of Fauquier County was captured, while Sergeant Solomon Fitzpatrick was wounded and taken prisoner. Their experiences testify to the close-quarters combat that ensued once the British closed in.[16]

The 15th Virginia included many men from the state's tidewater and southeastern counties. Few accounts from unit members have survived. Among its ranks, Private Timothy O'Conner was wounded above the left ankle and later taken prisoner, while Private Richard Taylor was wounded in the right leg.[17]

Thomas Ruter, a fifer from Nansemond County, stood five feet, ten inches tall (about average for a man of the period) and had brown hair. As a musician he played a critical role in communicating battlefield commands. Ruter survived the battle unscathed.[18]

Woodford's brigade, the largest on the American line, would have been firing over two thousand rounds at the British every minute once the 3rd Virginia rejoined them. Combined with Scott's troops, it was an impressive amount of firepower, though the muskets could only hit a target about a hundred yards out. Nor could they maintain that rate of fire for long as muskets fouled and they received British fire. Nor would they want to use up all of their ammunition.

Deployed between Woodford's and Scott's brigades were two three-pound guns that gave good support to the infantry. With a

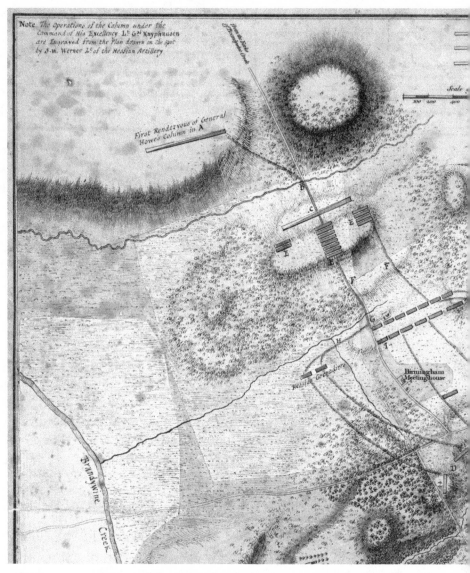

A detailed map of the Battle of Brandywine by William Faden, 1784. Note the Birmingham Meetinghouse labeled in the center. The description of the lettered references on the map reads: "The column under General Howe having crossed at 11 o'clock the first Branch of the Brandywine Creek at James Trimble Ford, halted at A. Continued its march at 2 o'clock, then crossed the other Branch of the Creek at B, and halted a second time at C to reconnoiter the position of the Enemy which was posted at DDD. The General formed Three Columns EEE having left the third Brigade on the height to cover the Equipage. At 4 o'clock in the afternoon the Three Columns advanced by F, and the

Middle Column being arrived in G; the Brigade of Hessian Grenadiers under the command of Colonel Donop was detached by H. This column having developed itself in I the general attack began..—The Enemy was forced to leave the Field of Battle and to retire by KKK being briskly pursued: but perceiving the Second Battalion of English Grenadiers without support, some of the Flying Brigades rally'd in LL and fell upon that Battalion in M. The Fourth Brigade came to the assistance of the Grenadiers and the Enemy, after obstinate defence was forced to Fly again, and the affair was decided."
(*Library of Congress*)

maximum range of about 3,200 feet, they could hit targets far out in front, though they could not see beyond the woods to their north. The approaching British and German troops had cover from the trees and low ground as they closed in.

Lieutenant Colonel Samuel Smith of the 4th Maryland wrote that "Woodford's Capt. of Artillery and 3 Lieutenants were wounded and more than half of the men killed." In addition, "the horses were shot down," essentially stranding the guns. Here the Americans lost two guns, which the British were no doubt glad to claim as trophies, considering the havoc they had caused them.[19]

Private John Oliver, serving in Scott's Virginia Brigade, was wounded in the thigh. Nearby, Glover Baker of the 4th Virginia was wounded in the wrist and had two bones broken. William Fife, described as a large man, stood in the rear rank as they blazed away at the British. Despite being in the back of the line, Fife was hit in the shoulder.[20]

Peter Cartwright from Amherst County, also serving in the 4th Virginia, lost two brothers that afternoon. John Nix of Winchester saw his brother Francis, a sergeant, killed in the action.[21]

In the 8th Virginia's line, Private James Kay was wounded in the hand. Nearby, William Jones had a British musket ball pass through his knee, fracturing the bones. The 8th Regiment of Scott's brigade were largely from the western and frontier counties, including land that later was ceded to Pennsylvania. Most of these troops wore hunting frocks and frontier garb.[22]

Thirty-year-old David Williams of the 8th Virginia was shot through the leg and gruesomely hit in the face, with part of his jaw and several teeth carried away. Yet the soldier from Virginia's frontier region survived the ordeal and the war.[23]

William Moody of the 8th Regiment was wounded in the left arm and on the head. Thomas Watson, a twenty-three-year-old soldier from Berkeley County, was fighting in his first battle and was wounded in the shoulder. Private John Valentine was wounded in the ankle and foot, disabling him for life.[24]

In the 12th Virginia's ranks, Private John Bray was wounded but escaped, and Vincent Tapp was struck in the arm. Daniel Flynn was hit in the head by a ball and described it years later as a "dangerous wound."[25]

James Ball, a twenty-eight-year-old soldier in the 12th Regiment, was wounded twice. George Black, an eighteen-year-old private, was "severely wounded" and captured. Black's thigh was broken by a musket ball, but he survived the ordeal.[26]

Robert Beckham of Chesterfield County near Richmond was wounded in the head and lost the use of his right eye afterward. James Reddin survived unscathed but recalled seeing Private Thomas Galford wounded by a ball in the knee. Up to that point, Galford had fought bravely under fire and "distinguished himself" in the opinion of Reddin.[27]

The 12th Virginia was heavily engaged, as numerous accounts of wounds and battle details testify. Fighting along the crest above Sandy Hollow, the troops stood their ground and took a terrible punishment from the British Light Infantry opposing them.

Private William Beale was wounded in the forehead, but the twenty-five-year-old survived. Joshua Younger was wounded in the ranks, and Private Isaac Jackson recalled that he fired eighty rounds of ammunition, an incredibly high number. Most cartridge boxes held about twenty or thirty rounds, so soldiers like Jackson were resupplied during the fighting, though when or how he does not say.[28]

Unlike the 8th and 12th Regiments, most of the men in Grayson's Additional Continental Regiment wore blue coats trimmed with red. Captain Cleon Moore of Grayson's Regiment was wounded in the hip. James Robinson, a twenty-five-year-old private, was wounded in the left arm and hip.[29]

Brothers Luke and William Metheany, twenty-four and eighteen years old respectively, were both taken prisoner, as was Private Ludwick Miller. In addition, William was wounded in the left leg before being taken.[30]

Family tradition among descendants of Nahor Norris, a Virginia soldier, maintain that he fired until his musket burst in his hands. An officer riding by did not notice amid the noise of the firing and fifes, and Norris had to hold up his hands to show what had happened.[31]

In Patton's Additional Continental Regiment, Private John Stewart was wounded in the left arm and Private Jacob Cook shot in the right leg. Other losses for the unit are not known.[32]

Captain John Peebles, a grenadier from the British 42nd Regiment serving with the 2nd Battalion of British Grenadiers, wrote,

> The 1st and 2nd Light Infantry & some Yaugers on the left of the Guards on the right, 1st Grrs. On the left of the Guards, 2d Grrs. On the left of the 1st. & 4th Brigade on the left of the 2d Grrs.; these moved on in Columns for nearly half a mile when the Rebels were discover'd drawn up on an advantageous ground forming an extensive line, with Cannon on several hill. The British Troops formed their respective Corps & moved up to the Enemy under a heavy fire mostly from behind fences, & after giving them a few rounds charged.[33]

Lieutenant Feilitzsch Heinrich Carl Philipp of the Ansbach-Bayreuth Jaeger Corps wrote that,

> At once the army marched into battalion order. Our corps extended the line on the end of the left wing. At exactly four o'clock the battle began. The small arms fire was terrible, the counter-fire from the enemy, especially against us, was the most concentrated. All the battalions made the attack. The enemy had made a good disposition with one height after the other to his rear. He stood fast and was certainly four times as strong as we were. However, all the English and Hessians conducted themselves as they are well-known to do. They attacked with great strength and with the bayonet.

The Hessian and Anspach Jaegers were on the British army's far left flank, attacking toward Stephen's right flank, Woodford's brigade.[34]

A German Jaeger officer gave a good description of the rolling and wooded terrain's effect on the combat when he noted that they "were engaged for over half an hour, with grape shot and small arms, with a battalion of light infantry. We could not see the 2nd Battalion of Light Infantry because of the terrain, and while we re-

Born in Gibraltar, Captain John Montresor served with the Braddock expedition in 1755, then in other campaigns in the French and Indian War. This British engineer observed the fighting at Brandywine and provided an outstanding account from the British perspective. (*New York Public Library*)

ceived only a few orders, each commander had to act according to his own best judgement."[35]

The British 4th Brigade, originally deployed on the east side of Birmingham Road, drifted to the west side of the road as it advanced south. Thus it could not support the Jaegers and Light Infantry as intended.[36]

When Stirling's brigades under Conway and Dayton fell back, Stephen's troops under Scott and Woodford held out a bit longer. Woodford was hit in the hand by British artillery. Eventually both of the Virginia brigades were compelled to fall back and forced to leave behind two guns, many of the horses being hit. It was not possible to remove the cannons without the horses.[37]

Lieutenant Frederick Wethereill of the 17th Light Infantry noted, "The fire of Musquetry all this time was as Incessant & Tremulous, as ever had been Remember'd. . . . But the Ardour & Intrepidity of the Troops overcoming every Opposition & pressing on with an Impetuosity not to be resisted ... the Rebel Line incapable of further Resistance gave way in very part & fled with the utmost disorder."[38]

British captain and engineer John Montresor watched from the rear and rode over the contested ground after the fighting moved on. He wrote, "the ground on the left being the most difficult the rebels disputed it with the Light Infantry with great spirit, particularly their officers, this spot was a ploughed hill and they covered by its summit and flanked by a wood; however unfavourable the circumstances and ours was such that they pushed in upon [Stephen's Division] under a very heavy fire."[39]

Flanked on the left by Conway's withdrawal, Scott's Virginia brigade began to fall back. Yet, for a bit longer, Woodford's brigade held out on the far right. The men engaged here may not have been able to see that the rest of the troops to their left had withdrawn, as woods, and now smoke, would have blocked the view.[40]

General George Weedon, who brought up reinforcements later, wrote, "Woodford's Brigade stood firm & in good Order. . . . Woodford was wounded & more than half of his Men killed, but his two field Pieces would have been saved by the Extraordinary Exertions of the remaining Lieuts. with Lieut. Col. Febiger, Majr. Day, & Sergeant Majr. Broughton, but that the Horses were shot down, & they obliged to quit them—About 6 General Green's Division arrived to cover the Retreat, one of his Brigades [Weedon's] gave the Enemy such a check as produced the desired effect."[41]

The Jaegers were doing what they did best: moving forward through the broken terrain, picking out targets, using terrain to their advantage. Von Wurmb "had the call to attack sounded on the half moon [hunting horn jaegers carry], and the Jaegers, with the battalion of light infantry, stormed up the heights."[42]

On the far-left flank of Howe's advance, Captain Johann Ewald led sixty Jaegers on foot, fifteen mounted Jaegers, a company of the 42nd Highlanders under Captain McPherson, and a company of the 17th's Light Infantry led by Captain William Scott.[43]

Ewald described his view upon reaching the open ground in front of Woodford's brigade: "I gazed in astonishment when I got

General George Weedon served in the French and Indian War on the Virginia frontier. This experienced Virginia officer commanded a brigade that fought later in the action at Brandywine. (*New York Public Library*)

up the hill, for I found behind it—three to four hundred paces away—an entire line deployed in the best order, several of whom waved to me with their hats but did not shoot. I kept composed, examined them closely, rode back, and reported it at once to Lord Cornwallis by the Jaeger Hoffman." Here Ewald was observing the first American position before they fell back to the higher ground behind them to continue the fight.[44]

Ewald then wrote, "Now the enemy was boldly attacked along the entire line and driven back as far as Dilworthtown, after a steady, stubborn fight from hill to hill and from wall to wall." Obviously, the Americans made a few stands as they fell back to the southeast.[45]

Ewald wrote, "During the action Colonel Wurmb fell on the flank of the enemy, and Sergeant Bickell with six jaegers moved to his rear, whereupon the entire right wing of the enemy fled to Dilworthtown." These Germans got around Woodford's right flank to fire into the Americans' rear, hitting the depleted ranks of the 3rd Virginia.[46]

Lieutenant Martin Hunter of the 52nd Light Infantry noted, "They allowed us to advance till within one hundred and fifty yards of their line when they gave us a volley, which we returned, and then immediately charged. They stood the charge till we came to the last paling. Their line then began to break, and a general retreat took place soon after."[47]

A British officer in the 2nd Light Infantry Battalion, writing with creative punctuation, noted, "The first line attacked Instantly which the Enemy advance Line gave Way our army Still gained ground, although they had great Advantig of Ground and their Canon keep up a Constant fire on us. Yet We Ne'er Wass daunted they all gave way."[48]

A Hessian account stated, "the enemy retreated in confusion, abandoning two cannons and an ammunition caisson, which the Light Infantry, because they had attacked on the less steep slope of the height, took possession of."[49]

Colonel von Wurmb wrote that,

> . . . we found ourselves 150 paces from their line which was on a height in a woods and we were at the bottom also in the woods, between us was an open field. Here they fired on us with two cannon with canister and, because of the terrible terrain and the woods, our cannon could not get close enough, and had to remain to the right. Sergeant Bikell of Captain Wrenden's Company, who had the flanking battalion, moved left to a hill, where he inaccommodated the enemy for a half hour. Then we heard the firing to our right became lively and detected movements among the enemy whereupon we attacked them in God's Name and drove them from their post. As we were going up the hill, the English light infantry moved in 10 paces ahead of us and used the cannon, since we were very fatigued from the long march . . . we made no prisoners except for the severely wounded. Many dead lay to our front.[50]

A member of von Wurmb's Hessian Jaegers wrote of the latter part of the action that "The rough terrain caused the column to pull to the left and moved it away from the fighting."[51]

Major General Charles Grey. Grey had experience from the Seven Years' War in Europe. He commanded a brigade at Brandywine. He is notorious for launching a bayonet attack on the American camp at Paoli, a few weeks after Brandywine. (*Library of Congress*)

Lieutenant Martin Hunter of the 52nd Light Infantry wrote that the American artillerymen "defended to the last, indeed, several officers were cut down at the guns. The Americans never fought so well before, and they fought to great advantage."[52]

The elite troops of the British Grenadiers, Light Infantry, and Guards had led the attack and suffered heavily, especially among their officers. Fifteen Light Infantry officers fell that afternoon. A British report lists 33 men and 8 officers killed from those units, along with 189 men and 23 officers wounded. Among the casualties were four drummers. Musicians were important for relaying messages on the battlefield and were thus with the front-line units in battle. The Hessian and Anspach Jaegers lost a total of 8 killed and 38 wounded.[53]

The British unit with the highest losses that day was the 2nd Battalion British Grenadiers, who lost 83, while the 1st Battalion British Grenadiers suffered 70 casualties. These were the units who engaged Conway's stubborn Pennsylvania brigade. The Irish-born officer led his regiments capably that day.[54]

Among the Grenadiers and Light Infantry from the 15th Regiment were one lieutenant killed, two captains and one lieutenant wounded, and several men killed. This was typical, as the Grenadiers and Light Infantry bore the brunt of the fighting, while the regular line companies of the British infantry regiments were less, if at all, engaged.[55]

Washington himself was now on the scene, and General Nathanael Greene's reserve troops were arriving just in time. It was around 6 p.m. when Greene deployed General Peter Muhlenberg's brigade on the right and Weedon's to the left below Dilworth. These fresh troops temporarily blunted the attacking British, who were fatigued and losing their cohesion.

Civilian Joseph Townsend wrote of the aftermath,

> We remained on the hill for some time, and when the engagement appeared to be nearly over . . . I proposed to some of my companions that we should go over to the field of battle and take a view of the dead and wounded. . . . We hastened thither and awful was the scene to behold—such a number of fellow beings lying together severely wounded, and some mortally—a few dead, but a small proportion of them considering the immense quantity of powder and ball that had been discharged. It was now time for the surgeons to exert themselves, and [many] of them were busily employed. Some of the doors of the meeting house were torn off and the wounded carried thereon into the house to be occupied for an hospital.[56]

It is interesting that this civilian with no military knowledge noted an important fact about Revolutionary War combat: casualties were small in comparison to the amount of ammunition expended on the battlefield.

The Brigade of Guards, on the British army's far right flank, continued its advance after driving off the Maryland brigades. They advanced over rolling terrain directly south, where they engaged other American troops overlooking Chad's Ford. Here they tied in with General Knyphausen's column, attacking across the Brandywine River. Thus the Guards became separated from the Hessian and British Grenadiers, who pursued the retreating forces of Ster-

American troops retreated at Brandywine in disorganization, with some still fighting while others fled. (*National Park Service*)

ling's division southeasterly. The 1st Battalion of the British Grenadiers became separated from the 2nd in the pursuit, with the 2nd moving down to and beyond Dilworth.

As the British troops advanced, the 4th Brigade came up to join in the front line, fighting below Dilworth. The 3rd Brigade followed up, keeping in the rear. Among its officers was thirty-year-old Captain John Andre, an aide to General Grey of the 3rd Brigade. Andre would later conspire with Benedict Arnold as his British point of contact and was captured and hung as a spy in 1780 in New York.[57]

Lieutenant William Hale of the 2nd Battalion British Grenadiers recalled how his men "drove them from six successive railings under an exceeding heavy fire . . . the battle continued for about three miles."[58]

His fellow officer, Captain Lieutenant John Peebles wrote of the fighting that moved beyond Birmingham Hill: "Our Troops pursued the fugitives thro' the woods & over fences for about 3 miles,

when they came upon a second & more extensive line of the Ene-
mys best Troops drawn up & posted to great advantage, here they
sustain'd a warm attack for some time & pour'd a heavy fire on the
British Troops as they came up, who were by this time much fatigued . . . notwithstanding these disadvantages we briskly attack'd
ye enemy & after a close fire for some minutes charged them again
& drove them."[59]

The action continued as a running battle down to Dilworth and
beyond, where Americans made a few brief stands. Along the
Wilmington Road General Nathanael Greene's troops formed a
final line at around seven o'clock. Then, with darkness approaching
and exhaustion setting in, the British pulled back and the battle
ended. The victorious army occupied the ground that night, while
Washington directed a retreat to the east.

The preceding chapter was as detailed as possible, using as many
eyewitness accounts as could be found. Yet how many crucial details
are we missing? How many experiences and observations went un-
recorded? Consequently this is a mere fraction of the incidents
which occurred on Birmingham Hill. It is the reality that our understanding of the most intense part of one of the largest engagements of the war will likely always be lacking.

Chapter 6

AFTERMATH

"A sore trial."
—John Matthews, 3rd Virginia

BRITISH SURGEONS TREATED THE WOUNDED that evening and into the following day, with more passing away from their wounds. The next day the British buried the dead of both sides, though no details mention where the graves were located.[1]

Some British and German troops who died from wounds were buried in the Birmingham Meeting House cemetery. The sturdy stone building was used as a hospital following the battle. Many private homes, barns, and Quaker meeting houses in the area were pressed into service. Wounded American soldiers who made it off the battlefield were taken to places such as Bethlehem or Litiz, where civilians were willing to care for them.

The Continental Army lost about 300 killed, 600 wounded, and 400 captured, for a total loss of around 1,300 out of 17,000 engaged. British and German forces lost 93 killed, 488 wounded, and 6 missing, totaling 587 out of 15,800 engaged. Some Hessian accounts place the army's losses higher, however. The bulk of all of those casualties occurred on Birmingham Hill.[2]

This plaque erected in 1915 at the Birmingham Meeting House notes its use as a hospital after the battle. Private homes all over the area were also appropriated for hospitals. (*Author*)

In the Continental Army the heaviest losses of the day were in Stephen's and Sterling's divisions. Sullivan also lost heavily, with the 1st Maryland Regiment losing around thirty men, and the 6th Regiment about as many. Conway's Pennsylvanians lost many officers; the 3rd Virginia lost about 60 of 170, over one third of their strength. Its chaplain and surgeon, Dr. David Griffith, noted that four officers were wounded and three killed. The British also captured fifteen brass cannons.[3]

An important question that cannot be answered with certainty is how long the fight at Birmingham Hill—the main part of the Battle of Brandywine—lasted. Stirling's report of an hour and forty-five minutes is surely too long. Several British accounts speak of it happening in a matter of minutes.

Two New Jersey officers, Dayton and Elmer, note that they deployed at about three or four o'clock. Two Hessian Jaeger accounts

The marker dedicated in 1920 for a mass grave of unknown British, German, and American troops who died during the Battle of Brandywine is in the Birmingham Meeting House cemetery. (*Author*)

claim that they attacked at four o'clock. Given variances between individual observations, somewhere between three and four o'clock seems a reasonable estimate for the British and German attack to have started.

Marshall claims that the 3rd Virginia stood for forty-five minutes in the orchard at the battle's start before falling back. That seems too long, for then he would not be retreating to the main line until about 4:15 p.m. or later, and by then the main American line along the crest was engaged.

Private Achilles Stapp of the 7th Virginia noted that he fired twenty-two rounds that afternoon, a significant number. In sustained combat, muskets will foul and become harder to load, and flints will lose their sharp edge, causing men to pause to do maintenance during the battle. Thus it is not realistic to estimate the length of engagement by this account, but it does speak to the intensity of the fighting. Firing at a rate of three shots a minute would take over seven minutes, but that cannot account for pausing to change flints, wipe out a dirty pan, or open a clogged touchhole. The rate of fire would also slow from changes in positioning, fouling in the barrel, and the musket becoming hot.[4]

FOLLOWING THE BATTLE there were engagements at Paoli and a few other sites. In late September the British captured Philadelphia. Washington struck back in early October at Germantown, a hard-fought battle that the Americans nearly won. The British spent the winter in Philadelphia while the Americans settled on Valley Forge for their winter encampment.

Brandywine had important and far-reaching consequences for the administrative history of the main army. Troublesome foreign officers like Conway and de Borre would not survive long in the Continental Army, and many of them were either dismissed or reassigned, or, desiring faster promotion, they left the service. The high casualties suffered by already weakened regiments also made reorganization necessary. Losses of even 20 or 30 men in a regiment that had only 150 to begin with were devastating.

This was also Lafayette's first battle, and he always looked back fondly on his experiences at Brandywine. In his 1824 visit to the United States, he indicated where he was wounded along the crest of the hill. In 1895, local citizens placed a monument to him nearby on the Birmingham Road at the highest point in the area. Later another monument to Lafayette and to Casimir Pulaski (a newly arrived Polish volunteer) was dedicated near the Birmingham Meeting House.

Lastly, the training put in place by von Steuben intended to correct many of the maneuvering and fighting deficiencies of troops that had not fought or trained together with one system. The Continental Army simply could not continue as it was and expect to defeat the British. Brandywine exposed a flurry of inefficiencies in the Continental Army's training, and while it was a frustrating defeat for Washington, it was a major turning point for how the army would function for the remainder of the war

Valley Forge, a hallowed place in American history. The Continental Army spent the winter of 1777-78 here. The winter was not terribly bad, as often thought, but supply problems were rampant. The army's training under von Steuben was the most important result of the encampment. (*Author*)

The new von Steuben Manual, implemented later at Valley Forge, simplified and combined steps for loading. For example, the command "Shoulder Your Firelock!" simply became "Shoulder Firelock!" Instead of "Make Ready, Present, Give Fire!" the commands became "Ready, Aim, Fire!" Von Steuben reduced the steps for loading from nineteen to fifteen.[5]

Not only was the new manual simpler, but it was also adopted as the official manual for the entire army. Once all of the troops learned it, better coordination was possible. The tangible results would be seen later in June 1778 at the Battle of Monmouth. In this engagement the Americans deployed and fought well, applying the training they learned under von Steuben.

The army was not incompetent at Brandywine, and the manual of von Steuben should not be overstated. The troops were gaining a measure of experience and fought well at Brandywine. It was a step in their process of development, but one that requires deeper examination.[6]

At Brandywine, the different units of the Continental Army had never coordinated on this scale before, having only fought in smaller battles in New Jersey. Many of the units used different manuals for drill and maneuver, so units could not act in concert. On the battlefield it was critical for regiments to maneuver, load, and fire in concert.

Recognizing the deficiencies that training with multiple drill manuals created for his army, Washington wrote at the end of the campaign his desire for "establishing one uniform sett of Manoeuvres and Manual."[7]

This would occur that winter at Valley Forge when Baron von Steuben brought a uniform drill to the army. From then on, the army marched, maneuvered, loaded, and fired using a single system. The importance of the training provided by von Steuben at Valley Forge in the spring of 1778 has been well covered by authors and historians. Yet the obvious deficiencies displayed in combat at Brandywine have not been fully appreciated for their role in the American defeat.

The failure of the British to crush the rebellion and end it shortly allowed the American forces to gain a measure of confidence and experience, which was refined and built on by von Steuben. Perhaps Hessian Colonel von Donop said it best when he wrote, "We have allowed the rebels too much time in which to become soldiers." Although a defeat, the Americans had fought well, and they knew it.[8]

Virginia General George Weedon summed up the growing sense of competence and confidence after Brandywine, writing, "Such disappointments as these tryes the Philosophy of a man and happy is he who is so much a pridestarian as to suppose it is all for the best."[9]

General Washington, no doubt exhausted by the day's events, wrote to Congress at midnight from Chester: "Notwithstanding the misfortunes of the day, I am happy to find the troops in good spirits and I hope another time we shall compensate for the losses now sustained." This optimism is expressed in many participant accounts, including both Continental officers and soldiers.[10]

Strict discipline and strong esprit de corps gave British troops a decided advantage for much of the first part of the war. At nearly all levels the British infantry were well led. (*National Park Service*)

The battle surely haunted General John Sullivan for the rest of his days. In the aftermath he wrote extensively, defending his actions. In fact, a member of Congress questioned his actions publicly. It does seem that Sullivan did all he could given the circumstances: a fluid situation, untested commanders, and units which had never maneuvered together. He was later court martialed but cleared of wrongdoing or misjudgment. Washington never doubted him at Brandywine, and Sullivan later held important commands.[11]

The Battlefield of Brandywine, a mid-eighteenth-century engraving. (*New York Public Library*)

Chapter 7

REMEMBERING

"Franco-American friendship is to last forever."
—French Ambassador Jean Jusseraud, 1915

UNLIKE THE GREAT BATTLEFIELDS of the Civil War, Revolutionary War sites were not preserved as battlefield parks until the historic preservation movement was well underway in the twentieth century. In the late nineteenth century, Civil War veterans were a powerful political group who held reunions and lobbied to commemorate their actions. These conditions did not exist for Revolutionary veterans in the antebellum years.

There was local interest in the battle, however, and several monuments and cannons were placed to commemorate the engagement. In 1877, the hundredth anniversary of the battle, a cannon was installed marking the fighting above Sandy Hollow. That year, on September 11, local militia units from Pennsylvania and Delaware gathered at the battle site, camping on the grounds at the Ring House, Washington's headquarters. The troops drilled for the public and fired salutes, and the highlight was a "sham battle," or reenactment. The participants could remake history to their liking, as a newspaper reported, "The American forces were not routed at the battle of Brandywine yesterday." Local politicians gave

Located not where he was wounded but on high ground along the Birmingham road, this monument honors Lafayette and his role in the battle. Local residents placed it here in 1895. (*Author*)

patriotic speeches, and special excursion trains brought visitors to Chad's Ford.[1] Why the participants chose to mark Sandy Hollow and not Birmingham Hill is not clear. Commemorations over the succeeding decades were irregular.

The next major celebration was held on September 11, 1895. The highlight was an effort by Chester County schoolchildren helping to fund a marble monument to Lafayette. It was a huge affair, with five thousand attending the ceremony. Placed along Birmingham Road, it is about a quarter mile from the spot where he was actually wounded. The monument is an impressive Corinthian column, with a laurel wreath and a band of thirteen stars. Topped with a cannonball, it includes a quote of Lafayette on his wounding in the battle.[2]

The Frenchman himself had visited in 1824 during his triumphal American tour and pointed out the spot where the Penn-

One of two Civil War-era cannons placed on the battlefield in 1900. The cannons mark the location of an American artillery battery next to Conway's brigade on the crest of the hill. (*Author*)

sylvania troops were engaged west of Birmingham Road. As his first battle in American service, and a site where he was wounded, Brandywine had a special meaning to Lafayette.

In 1900 the local Grand Army of the Republic post (composed of Civil War veterans), installed two Civil War era naval cannons to mark the fighting above Sandy Hollow and another to note the American artillery position above Birmingham Hill. In the decades after the Civil War, veterans of both sides were active in commemorating Revolutionary War sites (Confederate veterans spearheaded efforts at Kings Mountain, South Carolina, for example). Veterans were also politically powerful, with many serving as state governors, congressmen, and presidents. Civil War veterans felt it important to commemorate historic events and locations, and this time period saw the establishment of many parks, battlefields, and historic sites.[3]

Next to the Birmingham Meeting House graveyard is the Lafayette Cemetery, with this imposing monument, left, to that general. The Taylor Monument, right, is one of several placed in a group in the Lafayette Cemetery. (*Author*)

Around this time, local citizens placed four impressive stone monuments in the heart of the battlefield in Lafayette Cemetery, adjacent to the Birmingham Meeting House. A monument to Lafayette and Pulaski was dedicated in 1900, funded by local banker John G. Taylor, who had an ancestor in the battle and took a personal interest in commemorating it.[4]

John Taylor in 1898 also placed a monument for his grandfather Isaac Taylor, who fought in the battle with Pennsylvania troops. In 1904 he also added a monument honoring General Anthony Wayne.

Captain Joseph McClellan fought with the 9th Pennsylvania along the crest of Birmingham Hill. Dedicated in 1895 by his descendants, his monument stands not far from where he fought in 1777.[5]

As there was no battlefield park, the cemetery was the natural place to put monuments. It was also a spot where visitors could tour the battlefield and stop to see a landmark, the meeting house.

The Capt. John McClellan Monument. Dedicated by a descendant in 1895, it stands in the Lafayette Cemetery. (*Author*)

Commemorative efforts in the 1910s coincided with the rise in auto touring. In 1915 the Commonwealth of Pennsylvania launched a battlefield driving tour. The state placed small metal markers at key sites along area roads, identifying marching routes and battle locations. This was done without preserving any land, so visitors followed the route through private property. There was also much less traffic on the narrow country roads in 1915 than in 2020, making it much safer to casually drive and pull over.

A large commemoration on September 11, 1915, included local historical societies, the governor, senators, and representatives from England and the French ambassador. The ceremony was held at the Birmingham Meeting House, and the historic markers officially dedicated. The event included displays of artifacts found on the battlefield, and many local patriotic groups, some dressed in historic clothing, were present. An estimated three thousand people attended.[6]

Top: The monuments in Lafayette Cemetery are all in a row near the entrance. The 3rd Virginia defended this ground at the start of the battle. Bottom: In 1915, the state of Pennsylvania placed small markers around the area to mark important battlefield land-marks, essentially creating the first driving tour of the battlefield. This one is on Osborne Hill. Many still remain, though they are not always at convenient places to stop. (*Author*)

With the Great War raging in Europe, there was a great deal of public sympathy for France and her suffering, and organizers naturally drew a connection with Brandywine, it being Lafayette's first battle (and where he shed blood for the Americans).

The commemoration, consistently called a celebration, was the largest gathering of people in Birmingham Township since the battle. Held against the backdrop of the World War in Europe, that topic was referred to numerous times by reporters, speakers, and participants. The United States was still neutral, not entering for another two years.[7]

In 1927 a pageant in Dilworth commemorated the battle's 150th anniversary. Pageants were wildly popular in these decades, and often these events commemorated historical events.

Two decades later, in 1947, the Commonwealth of Pennsylvania created Brandywine Battlefield Park, acquiring only fifty acres that included the Gilpin House (Lafayette's headquarters) and ruins of the Ring House (Washington's headquarters). No significant fighting took place here, however.[8]

The local Chad's Ford Historical Society, formed in 1968, has also preserved important areas of the battlefield. Its first acquisition was the 1725 John Chad House. Not only was the home the community's namesake, it was the site of an American artillery position. The society then purchased and restored the 1714 Barns-Brinton House on another part of the battlefield. Many of these efforts were tied to the upcoming bicentennial of the Revolution, when communities across the nation began actively preserving and interpreting historic sites.

The battlefield—the entire area where troops fought—covers over ten square miles (thirty-five thousand acres) in parts of two counties, and had it been preserved along the lines of other battlefield parks it would be as sprawling as the parks at Manassas or Antietam. Although there was interest in marking the battle site and identifying key areas, there was not a movement to preserve Brandywine as a park along the lines of the Civil War sites.

Historic preservation has evolved over time, from placing monuments in the early stages, to preserving tracts of land where battles

Lafayette used the Gilpin House for his headquarters, not far from the Ring House used by Washington. Today the house is preserved by the state historic park. (*Author*)

were fought. This trend is illustrated at Brandywine, as its first preservation efforts focused on placing monuments and cannons. In recent years land has been set aside and interpreted for public visitation and understanding.

In 2002 Birmingham Township (part of Chester County) established Sandy Hollow Heritage Park (though this ground is part of Birmingham Hill, and Sandy Hollow itself is to the south). This preserved a pristine and key part of the battlefield, where Woodford's and Scott's Virginia brigades fought. The forty-two acres includes a one-mile walking trail and interpretive markers.[9]

The township created the Birmingham Hill Footpath in 2009. This borders land preserved by the Brandywine Conservancy for easement and includes a one-mile walking trail that covers ground crossed by the British Grenadiers in their attack on Dayton's and Conway's brigades. Full-color historic markers with maps provide interpretation of the events here.

Together, these two areas preserve separate but valuable core areas of the battlefield, which are both pristine. They serve as a

Top: Sandy Hollow Park actually preserves battlefield land on the eastern side of Birmingham Hill; Sandy Hollow is to the south. The park includes a walking trail and historic markers. Bottom: The Birmingham Hill area with a walking trail and historic markers lies in the very center of the British Grenadier and Light Infantry advance against Conway's Pennsylvanians. The preservation of this ground allows one to walk the attack route and understand the key terrain here. (*Author*)

basis from which future preservation could grow, encompassing more of the heart of the battlefield.

Preservation picked up steam in the next decade. In 2011, Delaware County, which includes the latter parts of the battle, prepared a conservancy plan that addressed historic preservation, public access to sites, and on-site interpretation. The plans sought public input in how best to preserve the sites and make them accessible, as well as detailed maps.[10]

For two decades the Civil War Trust had been successfully preserving battlefield land from that conflict with tremendous success. In 2014 the trust formed Campaign 1776 to begin preserving Revolutionary War sites as well. Now rebranded as the American Battlefield Trust, the organization has worked diligently to save land at many sites from the Revolution and the War of 1812 as well.

In 2017, the trust purchased its first land at Brandywine, including a small tract at Birmingham Hill and ten acres behind Sandy Hollow. As of 2020 the trust has also saved eighty-eight acres at Osborne's Hill.

In 2020, several groups came together to preserve another seventy-two acres just south of the main area of fighting, known as the Brinton Run Preserve. The American Battlefield Trust, Delaware County, Chad's Ford Township, the North American Land Trust, and the Land Conservancy for Southern Chester County all contributed to the effort. Future plans for the site include walking trails and interpretive markers.[11]

Although not preserved as a battlefield park during the golden age of battlefield preservation of the late nineteenth century, Brandywine started to get the attention it deserves in the early twenty-first century, using new strategies of land preservation that were not available in previous eras. It is hoped that with greater appreciation for the significance of the battle and the intensity of the combat, more of Brandywine will be preserved in the future. The potential exists to save more land and better interpret these events.

THE ARMIES

"Let us have a Respectable Army."
—General George Washington, 1775

THE FOLLOWING SECTION EXPLORES the recruitment, training, and experience of the three Continental divisions that fought at Birmingham Hill, so as to understand how they differed and how those differences played into what unfolded. These three divisions had never fought together side by side as they were about to. Moreover, Washington and his officers were still building a sense of nationalism in the Continental Army.

Continental Army regiments had an authorized strength of 738 officers and men, though most never recruited fully to that strength or kept it for long. Illness, transfers, desertion, and active campaigning reduced most units at Brandywine to about two hundred men.

Stirling's division of two brigades included Brigadier General Thomas Conway's 3rd Pennsylvania Brigade and Brigadier General William Maxwell's New Jersey Brigade (led by Colonel Elias Dayton). Conway was an Irish-born volunteer, one of the many foreigners who were starting to become a nuisance to General Washington. Later Conway was to prove himself quarrelsome and stubborn but handled his troops well in the battle. He led four regiments, the 3rd, 6th, 9th, and 12th Pennsylvania.[1]

Conway drilled his troops, and the brigade was probably one of the better ones to fight at Brandywine. Chevalier Dubuysson, cousin of Lafayette, had travelled with him to America to fight in the Revolution and described Conway's training: "M. de Conway, brigadier general, is detested by the officers of his brigade and envied by all the generals, including Washington, because he makes his brigade work and personally drills and instructs it, instead of leaving idle in camp." While the men may not have appreciated Conway's discipline, it would pay off at Birmingham Hill.[2]

The 3rd Pennsylvania Regiment (the nucleus of which was the 2nd Pennsylvania Battalion) was apparently poorly equipped, with a mixture of old brown and newer blue coats. This was probably true of most of Conway's men, except for the 12th Pennsylvania. The 3rd Regiment contained men from Northumberland, Northampton, Westmoreland, Berks, and Philadelphia, a mix of settlers from the frontier amid the more settled southeastern area of the state. Most of these counties were larger than their present-day namesakes. Northumberland, for example, included parts of twenty modern central Pennsylvania counties. Under the command of Colonel Thomas Craig, the 3rd had 150 men present on September 11.[3]

The 3rd Regiment was organized in December 1776 and was thus a new unit for the spring and summer New Jersey campaigns. Many of its men, however, were veterans from the old 2nd Pennsylvania Battalion, which was disbanded. Its weakness, however, would be in fighting a battle as large as Brandywine.[4]

The 6th Pennsylvania, under Lieutenant Colonel Josiah Harner, was raised largely from Lancaster and Chester Counties, although a few western settlers from Bedford and Northumberland County were mixed in. Many of the regiment's men were veterans from the disbanded 5th Pennsylvania Battalion, with a sprinkling of newer recruits. Like most of the Continental troops at this time, the 6th seems to have been outfitted in brown coats faced with red. Some of the men also wore hunting shirts and leather breeches.[5]

Like the 3rd, many of the men in the 6th Regiment were veterans, having fought in the now disbanded 5th Pennsylvania Battalion. The 6th was organized in January 1777, so like the 3rd it only had small-action experience.[6]

The 9th Pennsylvania was an older unit, unlike the previous two, which were recruited and organized earlier that year. Their coats, for those who had them, were brown faced with red. The 9th's companies were raised in Cumberland, Philadelphia, Bucks, Lancaster, York, and Berks Counties, as with the other regiments a good mix of easterner and westerner. Data suggests that many foreign-born men served in its ranks, especially Irish, Scottish, English, and German. This was probably pretty typical of many of these Pennsylvania units. Major Francis Nichols led them at Brandywine.[7]

The 9th Regiment fought in New Jersey in the spring and summer of 1777, and its largest battle before Brandywine would have been Short Hills, as part of a two-brigade force. It is estimated to have about 239 men at Brandywine.[8]

Next was the 12th, which was also an older regiment. Companies B, C, D, and E were raised in Northumberland County, G from Northampton, while the balance were from Berks and other eastern areas. Many of the men were armed with rifles and the unit was often employed in skirmishing. Not surprisingly, the unit also seems to have been poorly supplied with uniforms, most men wearing civilian clothes. It was Conway's largest unit with 231 men under the command of Colonel William Cooke.[9]

Completing Conway's brigade was Colonel Oliver Spencer's New Jersey Regiment, consisting of 186 men. Organized in the spring at Monmouth, its men were from New Jersey and one company hailed from Pennsylvania.[10]

Conway's regiments had served together for much of 1777 and had a certain amount of cohesion. Many of them had combat experience from other campaigns as well. These would be the only Pennsylvania troops involved in the fierce fighting on their home soil at Birmingham Hill.

Stirling's other brigade under Colonel Elias Dayton had four New Jersey Regiments: the 1st, 2nd, 3rd, and 4th. The 1st and 3rd Regiments had seen action in the Lake Champlain theater and only recently had rejoined the main army. The 3rd New Jersey was outfitted with tan coats faced with blue. Many had buckskin breeches and buff leather crossbelts and cartridge boxes. Most of the New Jersey troops were armed with American-made contract muskets, copies of the British Brown Bess.[11]

Earlier in the summer, the New Jersey Brigade had been split, with the 2nd and 4th Regiments operating separately from the 1st and 3rd. It has been assumed by earlier historians, including Samuel S. Smith in his excellent book, that the units were not re-united by the time of Brandywine. Yet records indicate that in fact they were, and all four units fought at Birmingham Hill.

The 1st New Jersey had men from Middlesex, Morris, Somerset, Monmouth, Essex, and Bergen Counties. These men had seen a great deal of action in their native state that spring and summer. Colonel Mathias Ogden led them at Brandywine. The 1st New Jersey had 184 men.[12]

The 2nd New Jersey was organized in October 1775 at Burlington and Trenton. Its men were from Burlington, Gloucester, Salem, Sussex, and Hunterdon Counties. The unit had fought in the Forage War and at Short Hills before arriving in Pennsylvania. It had 310 men at Brandywine.[13]

Organized in Elizabethtown in the late winter of 1776, the 3rd New Jersey had under three hundred troops at Brandywine. Colonel Elias Dayton was the unit's commander. Colonel Ephraim Martin led the 4th New Jersey, which saw action with its sister regiments in its home state. At Brandywine it had 266 men in the ranks.[14]

General Maxwell normally commanded the New Jersey Brigade but had recently been assigned to lead the newly formed light infantry brigade. Command of the Jersey regiments then fell to Colonel Dayton.[15]

General Adam Stephen's division included the 3rd and 4th Virginia Brigades, under Brigadier Generals William Woodford and Charles Scott respectively. Woodford's command consisted of the 3rd, 7th, 11th, and 15th Virginia Regiments. Most of these troops were combat veterans who would be put to the test this day.

The 3rd Virginia included many prominent names on its officer's roll, including George Weedon (who was promoted to brigadier general), James Monroe (a future president), William Washington (cousin of the commanding general and later a cavalry commander in the South), Thomas Marshall (his son John, future Supreme Court chief justice, was serving in the 11th Virginia that day), and members of the prestigious Lee family. Its companies had been raised in Westmoreland, Spotsylvania, King George, and other counties in the Fredericksburg area. The unit distinguished itself at Trenton and Princeton (where Hugh Mercer, another prominent officer, was killed). The men of this unit initially wore blue hunting frocks, and some had light blue coats by 1777. There were 170 men in the unit.[16]

Next was the 7th Virginia, raised in the eastern counties of Gloucester Court House, King William, King and Queen, Middlesex, and Halifax, as well as the western regions of Chesterfield, Albemarle, Culpeper, Orange, and Botetourt. This large regiment had 472 men ready for duty. Most of the men wore dark (black) hunting frocks and brown leggings. Colonel Alexander McClanahan commanded the unit.[17]

The 11th Virginia is famous for serving under Colonel Daniel Morgan, one of the war's best combat leaders. At this time Morgan was with the Northern Army, but his influence could still be felt in the 11th (this day led by Lieutenant Colonel Christian Febiger). The regiment's 377 men were recruited in Prince William, Amelia, Loudon, and Frederick Counties, with a good mixture of frontier riflemen in its ranks. Many of the unit's officers had fought in the ill-fated Canadian invasion of 1776. The 11th is an ancestor of today's 201st Field Artillery, West Virginia National Guard.[18]

Rounding out Woodford's brigade was the 15th Virginia, the last authorized by the Virginia General Assembly and the highest-numbered regiment produced by the state during the war. Companies were recruited in Princess Anne, Nansemond, King William, Richmond, Westmoreland, Isle of Wight, Sussex, Southampton, Surry, Brunswick, Amelia, Norfolk, and Chesterfield Counties. At least some troops wore blue coats faced with white.[19]

In Woodford's brigade, all of the regiments had a good deal of combat experience. Yet like the troops in the other brigades, they had never fought in an action as large as Brandywine.

Scott's brigade consisted of the 4th, 8th, and 12th Regiments, as well as Grayson's and Patton's regiments. The latter two had troops from Virginia, Maryland, Delaware, and Pennsylvania.

The 4th Virginia came largely from the Southside counties, those below the James River and bordering North Carolina. Its men hailed from the rural farming areas of Berkeley, Prince Edward, Charlotte, Southampton, Sussex, Brunswick, Isle of Wight, Surry, and Nansemond Counties. Many of these men wore hunting shirts.[20]

Companies for the 8th Virginia came from Augusta, Dunmore, Culpeper, Berkeley, Fincastle, Augusta, Hampshire, Frederick, and West Augusta, frontier areas at the time. West Augusta was the northwestern county of the state later ceded to Pennsylvania (the area around Pittsburgh). The regiment's flag consisted of salmon silk with a white scroll and the words "VIII Virga Regt." Its large number of ethnic Germans from the Shenandoah Valley and western mountains gave it the nickname, the German Regiment. These frontier soldiers mostly wore hunting frocks.[21]

The 12th also came from the frontier, being raised in the counties of Augusta, Hampshire, West Augusta, Botetourt, and Rockbridge. Many of the militia companies that comprised the basis for this unit had been serving in frontier garrisons and were skilled at combat with the Native Americans. As with the 8th Virginia, the men from West Augusta County were from land that was in dispute with Pennsylvania and that Virginia would in fact cede after the war. Many of these men had served in the Fort Pitt garrison until the spring of 1777 (modern Pittsburgh). The majority of these men also wore hunting shirts common on the frontier rather than military coats.[22]

Grayson's regiment, known officially as Grayson's Additional Continental Regiment, was raised in both Virginia and Maryland. Colonel William Grayson was regimental commander at Brandywine. The men wore blue coats trimmed with red, and some had hunting shirts.[23]

Patton's regiment, officially Patton's Additional Continental Regiment, included troops from Maryland, Pennsylvania, and Delaware. Colonel John Patton headed the unit. These unnumbered units named as "Additional Regiments" reflect a later round of recruitment after states had already sent regiments to join the Continental Army.[24]

The division commanded by Sullivan himself included some of the best combat units in the American army, the Maryland and Delaware troops. Sullivan had the 1st and 2nd Maryland Brigades, led by (most likely) Colonel John Hawkins Stone and General Preudhomme de Borre respectively.[25]

The commander of the 1st Maryland Brigade, Brigadier General William Smallwood, was absent on assignment, and the replacement commander is not known, though Colonel Stone was the senior colonel. Thus it is assumed, but cannot be proven, that Stone led the brigade. Smallwood was very experienced, having served in several battles up to this point and demonstrated his ability to lead troops through tough situations. His leadership would be sorely missed.

The 1st Maryland Brigade included the 1st, 3rd, 5th, and 6th Maryland and the Delaware Regiment. These were all combat veterans and had fought as a unit extensively. It may have been the best brigade in the entire army.[26]

The 1st Maryland Regiment consisted of companies from northern and western Maryland. (At this time all of central and western Maryland was part of Frederick County.) At a strength of two hundred men, it was the largest regiment in the brigade. Many of these men were probably experienced riflemen. These troops wore a mix of brown and blue coats faced with red. Their commander, Colonel John Hawkins Stone, left one of the best accounts of the action at Birmingham Hill. This unit had a great deal of experience, having served from the war's beginning.[27]

The 3rd Maryland Regiment was raised in March 1777 from men in Anne Arundel, Prince George's, Talbot, Harford, and Somerset Counties. Colonel Mordechai Gist, a talented officer, commanded this unit but had been sent with Smallwood on a recruiting drive. Lieutenant Colonel Nathaniel Ramsey led the 114 men of the regiment this day. These troops had a mix of blue coats faced with red and osnaburg hunting shirts. The 3rd Maryland, like the 1st, was a combat-hardened unit.[28]

The 5th Maryland was raised in Queen Anne, Kent, Caroline, and Dorchester Counties, on the eastern side of the Chesapeake Bay in early 1777. Only two of its companies were here at Brandy-wine, and their exact numbers are unknown. The unit wore brown coats trimmed in red, as well as civilian clothing. They were under the command of Captain Jesse Cosden. The 5th had joined the main army in May and had almost no combat experience.[29]

The last Maryland unit, the 6th, had been organized in Prince George's, Frederick, Cecil, Harford, Queen Anne, and Anne Arun-del Counties. The 6th stood out from her sister units, wearing a mix of brown and gray coats faced with green. These troops had joined the army in time to participate in the small-unit actions in New Jersey in the spring and summer of 1777.

The Delaware Regiment, the only one raised by this small state, matched its small numbers with an impressive reputation. Author-ized in 1775 as part of the original Continental Army, these troops fought with stubbornness at Long Island, White Plains, and would later do so in the Southern Campaign. The regiment's uniforms consisted of blue coats faced with white. Only seventy-nine of these veterans were on hand this day, led by Colonel David Hall.[30]

The 2nd Maryland Brigade also had veteran units but suffered under the inept leadership of de Borre, another foreign-born officer like Conway. His command consisted of the 2nd, 4th, 7th, and 8th Maryland and the 2nd Canadian Regiment.

The 2nd Maryland Regiment was organized from counties along the Chesapeake Bay and eastern Maryland. The men were attired in blue and brown coats faced with red, as well as brown and buff civilian coats. This was a veteran unit, having fought in New York and New Jersey since 1776.[31]

Next was the 4th Maryland, with companies raised in Baltimore, Anne Arundel, and Somerset Counties. These troops wore brown coats faced with red and osnaburg hunting shirts and leather breeches. Their commander was Colonel Josias Hall. The unit had not been at Trenton or Princeton but was in the spring and summer actions in New Jersey.[32]

The 7th Maryland, under Colonel John Gumby, had eight companies from Baltimore and Frederick Counties. Gumby would prove himself one of the war's better small-unit commanders. The men had blue coats faced with green, as well as gray faced with red. The men had fought in the spring and summer campaigns in New Jersey.[33]

The 8th Maryland, also known as the German Regiment for its high number of immigrants, was raised in Pennsylvania and Maryland. Five companies came from eastern Pennsylvania, two from Baltimore, and two from Frederick County. It thus had a large contingent of easterners joined by two frontier companies. While some of these men were second- or third-generation Americans, no doubt both German and English could be heard in the ranks. At least some of its men seem to have worn linen hunting shirts. This was by far the largest Maryland regiment, with just over three hundred men in the ranks, and led by Colonel Henry Arendt. The 8th saw its first action at Trenton and Princeton and had been with the army since.[34]

The 2nd Canadian Regiment, also known as Hazen's or Congress's Own, consisted of men from Montreal as well as the Richelieu and St. Lawrence River Valleys. While most French Canadians had adopted to English rule and opposed the rebellion, some joined the Americans in hopes of making Quebec the fourteenth colony to rebel. These French Canadians were joined by American settlers in Canada and upstate New Yorkers in forming two Canadian Regiments, units little known outside of Revolutionary scholarship today. Earlier in 1777 Maryland recruits had been added to its ranks. Colonel Moses Hazen, another excellent officer, led this unit. The men wore brown coats faced with white along with white waistcoats and breeches. Their caps had the abbreviation COR (Congress's Own Regiment). This was a good combat unit that would provide vital scouting duties in the day ahead. Its strength this day was nearly four hundred men.[35]

De Borre spoke very little English and showed little interest in learning. Despite his thirty-five years of experience in Europe, he brought little confidence to the army. He was among the many foreign volunteers arriving to assist the American cause, with mixed success.[36]

The American troops were heterogeneously armed and equipped. While many probably had regimental coats, some had the older brown pattern while others wore the newer blue. Even within regiments there was little consistency. These summaries are general descriptions only, as accurate details of what units wore are nonexistent. Most of these observations come from deserter advertisements and contemporary letters and reports.

The standard infantry weapons were imported French Charleville muskets or captured English Brown Bess muskets. Many troops also carried Committee of Safety Muskets, American-made copies of the British model. No doubt a good many men carried rifles, fowlers, and other arms as well. That spring over twenty-thousand French muskets were supplied to equip the army.[37]

The mixed armaments caused headaches for quartermasters and supply officers, since rifles and muskets, and different types of muskets, all required unique ammunition. In combat, riflemen could not load as quickly as soldiers with muskets. The various types of weapons also meant repair and issuing spare parts was complicated. Troops, even within a regiment, might be armed differently and could not maintain even rates of fire or be resupplied easily.

Not only was equipment irregular, but so was the training, discipline, and drill of these men. While some units were veteran, others were green. In addition, different regiments used different drill, or manuals. This caused complications, as troops marched, maneuvered, and loaded according to different commands. Some troops could maneuver and position themselves faster than others. Loading and firing rates were not consistent. It meant commanders had to wait for the slowest or most inexperienced unit to catch up or form. The problem would not be corrected until von Steuben stepped in at Valley Forge that winter. As historian Edward Lengel notes, the army was making significant improvement, and von Steuben's drill did not solve every problem, but it was a significant step forward.[38]

The defeat at Brandywine, and the difficulties encountered at Birmingham Hill, were due in large part to the poor command and control aspects of the American army. Many officers were still learning their trade; most had never led this many men in combat or were still settling into their roles of staff or support positions. In addition to lacking trained officers, being unskilled at complex maneuver, and lacking uniform regulations, the army was deficient in other areas too. The Continental forces lacked technical skills such as engineers, and intelligence gathering and analyzing.[39]

The large number of foreigners, while an infusion of experienced officers, was too much of a surge at once. The European officers, while experienced, could not relate to the American troops under their command. It also caused resentment among native-born officers and did not allow them to mature fully. Over forty French officers alone joined the army in the spring of 1777. Thus, inexperienced officers led a mix of green and veteran units.[40]

De Borre and Thomas Conway were examples of the flood of foreign officers arriving to help the American cause. It is no wonder that Congress and leaders like Washington were becoming skeptical of these foreign officers. Lafayette and von Steuben would be rare and pleasant exceptions. Conway later had his own problems when he criticized Washington and suggested he be replaced. When his opinions were made public, Conway resigned from the army.[41]

Over 1,800 post-war federal and state pension applications were reviewed for this study. Veterans of the war could obtain pensions from the federal government as well as their states, most in the 1810s or 1830s, or even later. Some documents contain important details of the battle not found anywhere else. A bit of statistical data can also be extracted from this source.

The majority of soldiers in the Continental Army at Brandywine were between eighteen and twenty-five years old, with the average age of twenty-two. Of the 1,800 pensions reviewed, over twenty were age fifteen or younger. Only a small number of soldiers were in their thirties, and very few were in their forties. A little more than half were illiterate.[42]

FACING THE THREE AMERICAN DIVISIONS at Birmingham Hill were troops under the command of Major General Charles Cornwallis. These 8,400 men in six brigades were all combat veterans. Despite a long flank march, they were professionals, and when the advance resumed, they went about their business with proficiency and skill.

They included Major General Charles Grey's 3rd Brigade (15th, 17th, 44th Regiments), Brigadier General James Agnew's 4th Brigade (33rd, 37th, 46th, and 64th Regiments), Brigadier General Edward Matthew's Brigade of Guards, the Light Infantry Brigade, the British Grenadier Brigade, Colonel Carl von Donop's Hessian Grenadier Brigade (von Linsingen, von Minnigerode, and Lengerke Battalions), and Lieutenant Colonel Ludwig von Wurmb's Jaegers (Hesse Cassel and Anspach-Beyreuth Jaegers).

The British and German forces used a complicated system to break down their units, so an explanation is in order. Each British regiment had eight regular companies and included a grenadier and a light infantry company. The grenadiers no longer carried grenades but retained their role as shock troops. They were the tallest and strongest men, wearing tall mitre caps. The authorized strength for a British regiment was 477 men, though most units were well below that at Brandywine.

Light infantry were trained in scouting and skirmishing and were thus more agile and flexible on the battlefield than the infantry in the regular companies. They wore small leather caps that identified them and were less cumbersome in wooded terrain.

British commanders often combined their grenadiers and light infantry companies into battalions, creating special shock troops from among their best units. Thus at Brandywine, General Howe had created two light infantry battalions, with all the light infantry companies drawn from the regiments, as well as a grenadier battalion. Of course the downside was that the regiments, down to eight companies from ten, also lost their best troops.

British infantry regiments wore red coats, but the facings of each regiment were different. Collars and cuffs were yellow, white, blue, black, or green, depending on the unit. This diversity in uniforms would be seen in the grenadier and light infantry battalions, composed of men drawn from various units but working together in concert.

British infantry regiments carried two flags into battle, a First Color, or King's Color, and a Second Color. The King's Color featured the Great Union: a red cross of St. George edged in white, with the diagonal white cross of St. Andrew on a field of blue. The Second Color was a regimental flag, with a small Union in the upper left corner (the hoist corner). The rest of the field included regimental symbols and often the number in Roman numerals. The flags were about six feet square and made of silk.

The 33rd Regiment, which saw action at Birmingham Hill, carried a King's Color with the Roman numeral "XXXIII" in the center. Their Second, or regimental, Color, was a red cross of St. George on a white field, with the Grand Union in the corner, and "Regt XXXII" surrounded by a wreath in the center.[43]

In addition to regular infantry regiments were the Brigade of Guards. The Guards were some of the most distinguished troops in the British army. There were three regiments of Foot Guards in London: the Grenadier Guards, Coldstream Guards, and Scots Guards. They provided security to the king and the royal family. A select detachment of these crack troops was sent to join the forces in America in 1776.

Upon arrival in British-held New York, they were organized into two battalions. The 1st Battalion consisted of the Grenadier Company (men and officers from all three regiments), the 1st, 2nd, and 3rd Infantry Companies (men and officers from Grenadier Guards), and the Brigade or 4th Company (men from all three Guards regiments).

The Second Battalion was composed of the 5th and 6th Companies (men and officers from Scots Guards), the 7th and 8th

Companies (from the Coldstream Guards), and a Light Infantry Company (men and officers from all three regiments). Thus, between their Guards Battalions, Light Infantry Battalions, and Grenadier Battalions, there was a considerable mixing of troops from different units in these new formations.

Two outstanding myths linger regarding the German troops that served in America with the British. First, they were not all Hessians. Germany was not a unified country, though the term "Germany" was in use at the time, referring to all the German-speaking states.

Several German nations, including Hesse-Cassel, Hesse-Hanau, Brandenburg, Hanover, Brunswick, Anspach, Bayreuth, Waldeck, and Anhalt-Zerbast contributed troops. The British military was stretched thin, and the additional troops augmented their forces in North America.

Secondly, these were not mercenaries. The individual soldiers had no say in the matter: as part of their nation's military, they were sent overseas. The soldiers were paid as all soldiers were through their government, and their prince or king received payment from the British government for the use of their troops.

The German units included infantry regiments with five companies: four line companies and one grenadier company. Rather than being numbered, they took the name of their commander, thus the von Linsingen or von Minnigerode Regiments.

The Germans also brought special units known as Jaegers, named for the German word for hunter. Jaegers wore green coats, carried rifles (rather than muskets), and were well trained in skirmishing and sharpshooting. They brought hunting traditions with them, including the use of a hunting horn to convey signals in battle. They also brought large-caliber rifles called amusettes, which required a two-man crew and were mounted on a swivel. Some Jaegers were game wardens or professional hunters, carried their own personal rifles, and were skilled marksmen.

German regular infantry units carried distinctive flags that would have stood out on the battlefield. Usually about four feet square with two layers of silk, they were often embellished with different decorations on the obverse and reverse sides. Each flag had symbols of its state. Hessian colors had a red and white striped lion, the symbol of Hesse, while Anspach-Beyreuth regiments had a red eagle, the symbol of Brandenburg.[44]

Some of these British and German troops saw action around Boston in 1775 and 1776, and all were involved with the battles around New York the year before. With German and British units operating closely in combat the obvious question is, how did they communicate? French was a common language that many European officers would have known, and there is evidence that German and English officers communicated in French.

It wasn't a perfect system, but it worked well enough. Adjutant General Major Carl Leopold Bauermeister of Hesse-Cassel, for example, noted that the English spoke poor French when communicating with them. But what about among small units like companies or battalions? Would mediocre command of a language suffice for communication in combat situations? Despite the many instances of German and British units mingling, there is precious little documentary evidence of how officers or common soldiers communicated. Perhaps they used a combination of French, translators who spoke either English or German, and hand signals or other agreed-upon methods. Timing and clarity are key in close-quarters combat; there is no chance to second guess in an ambush or a raid. There were likely instances of misunderstanding that may have led to mistakes and even led to friendly fire incidents.

ORDER OF BATTLE

Units involved at Birmingham Hill

CONTINENTAL ARMY

3rd Division—Maj. Gen. John Sullivan

    1st Maryland Brigade—commander unknown

        1st Maryland Regiment

        3rd Maryland Regiment

        5th Maryland Regiment

        6th Maryland Regiment

        Delaware Regiment

    2nd Maryland Brigade—Brig. Gen. Philippe Hubert de Borre

        2nd Maryland Regiment

        4th Maryland Regiment

        7th Maryland Regiment

        8th Maryland Regiment

        2nd Canadian Regiment

5th Division—Maj. Gen. William Alexander (Lord Stirling)

    New Jersey Brigade—Col. Elias Dayton

        1st New Jersey Regiment

        2nd New Jersey Regiment

        3rd New Jersey Regiment

        4th New Jersey Regiment

    3rd Pennsylvania Brigade—Brig. Gen. Thomas Conway

        3rd Pennsylvania Regiment

        6th Pennsylvania Regiment

        9th Pennsylvania Regiment

        12th Pennsylvania Regiment

        Spencer's Additional Regiment (NJ)

2nd Division—Maj. Gen. Adam Stephen
    3rd Virginia Brigade—Brig. Gen. William Woodford
        3rd Virginia Regiment
        7th Virginia Regiment
        11th Virginia Regiment
        15th Virginia Regiment
    4th Virginia Brigade—Brig. Gen. Charles Scott
        4th Virginia Regiment
        8th Virginia Regiment
        12th Virginia Regiment
Grayson's Additional Regiment (VA/MD)
Patton's Additional Regiment (MD/DE/PA)

BRITISH FORCES

Left Division—Maj. Gen. Charles Cornwallis
    3rd Brigade—Brig. Gen. Charles Grey
        15th Regiment
        17th Regiment
        44th Regiment
    4th Brigade—Brig. Gen. James Agnew
        33rd Regiment
        37th Regiment
        46th Regiment
        64th Regiment
    Light Infantry Brigade
        1st Battalion
        2nd Battalion
    British Grenadier Brigade
        1st Battalion
        2nd Battalion
    Hessian Grenadier Brigade—Col. Carl von Donop
        Von Linsingen Battalion
        Von Minnigerode Battalion
        Lengerke Battalion
        Hessian Jaegers
    16th Light Dragoons
    Royal Artillery

APPENDIX C

PRESERVATION

THERE ARE MANY WAYS to get involved and support Brandywine Battlefield Park and its educational mission and preserve more of the battlefield. The state historic park includes a museum and offers guided tours of Washington's and Lafayette's headquarters. It also hosts special events throughout the year and offers educational programs for school groups.

In addition to supporting the park's programs, there is a friends group (Brandywine Battlefield Park Associates) that partners with the park and provides assistance for its programs and initiatives. Joining the Brandywine Battlefield Park Associates is a more active way to support the park.

Finally, to support preservation of battlefield land, join or support the American Battlefield Trust. This group preserves Revolutionary, Civil War, and War of 1812 sites across the nation. As the 250th anniversary of the Revolution approaches (2025–2033), this is an excellent opportunity to save more land and support history education. It may be the last good chance to save significant areas of fighting. Nothing is more valuable and has a longer-lasting impact than the permanent preservation of battlefield land. The websites for the park and its friends group, and the trust, are: www.brandywinebattlefield.org and www.battlefields.org.

NOTES

INTRODUCTION

1. Herman Benninghoff, *Valley Forge: A Genesis of Command, Continental Army Style* (Gettysburg: Thomas Publications, 2001), 10.
2. John B.B. Trussell, *Birthplace of an Army* (Harrisburg: Pennsylvania Historical and Museum Commission, 1993), 56.
3. Ibid.
4. Michael Harris, *Brandywine* (El Dorado Hills, CA: Savas Beatie, 2014), 162, 190, 193; http://allthingsliberty.com/2014/05/the-25-deadliest-battles-of-the-revolutionary-war/, accessed December 11, 2014.
5. Mark Lender and James K. Martin, eds., *Citizen Soldier: The Revolutionary War Journal of Joseph Bloomfield* (Newark: New Jersey Historical Society, 1982), 127.

CHAPTER ONE: COMMAND AND CONTROL AND LINEAR COMBAT

1. Chauncey Ford, Worthington, ed., *The Writings of Washington*, Vol. XI (New York: Putnam Sons, 1890), 228-31; John Jackson, *Valley Forge: Pinnacle of Courage* (Gettysburg, PA: Thomas Publications, 1992), 128.
2. Ernest Peterkin, *The Exercise of Arms in the Continental Army* (Alexandria Bay, NY: Museum Restoration Services, 1989), 4; Marc Briar, Personal correspondence. Marc was a park ranger at Valley Forge National Historical Park with a great deal of knowledge about the campaign, weapons, and tactics.
3. Peterkin, 3-4.
4. Walter Henning, *The Statues at Large, Being a Collection of All the Laws of Virginia from the First Session of the Legislature, in the Year 1619*, Volume IX, p. 23, Accessible at http://vagenweb.org/hening/vol09-01.htm; Gustav Person, "I am no advocate for blindly following the maxims of European policy." American/European Training Manuals in the Era of the American Revolution. *The Continental Soldier* (Spring 2010), 10; Mike Jesberger email to author, January 9, 2015.
5. Joseph Lee Boyle, *Writings from the Valley Forge Encampment of the Continental Army* (Bowie, MD: Heritage Books, 2003), 133.
6. *Valley Forge Orderly Book of General George Weedon* (New Delhi: Isha Books, 2013), 305.

7. Peterkin, 4-5.

8. Ibid., 5.

9. Samuel Smith, *The Battle of Brandywine* (Monmouth Beach, NJ: Philip Freneau Press, 1976), 32.

10. Ibid., 29, 32.

CHAPTER TWO: THE BATTLE OF BRANDYWINE UNFOLDS

1. Joseph Townsend, "Some Accounts of the British Army under the Command of General Howe and the Battle of Brandywine," *Eyewitness Accounts of the American Revolution* (Arno Press and New York Times, 1969), 21.

2. Ibid., 23.

CHAPTER THREE: THE BATTLE DEVELOPS AT BIRMINGHAM HILL

1. https://storymaps.arcgis.com/stories/9cef8b93eaa94faf8e106edbb737ef1c. It has been speculated that Graves intended to open a store, as he listed so many items lost, more than a family would need. A store in fact opened on the site later in the nineteenth century.

2. Smith, 1.

3. Samuel White, Federal Pension Application, S 7871.

4. Otis G. Hammond, ed., *Letters and Papers of Major-General John Sullivan: Continental Army*, Vol. 1 (Concord, NH: New Hampshire Historical Society, 1930), 463-4.

5. Ibid.

6. Ibid., 464.

7. Harris, 289-90.

8. John Stone to William Paca, September 23, 1777, *The Chronicles of Baltimore, Being a Complete History of "Baltimore Town" and Baltimore City From the Earliest Period to the Present Time*, J. Thomas Scharf, ed. (Baltimore: Turnbull Brothers, 1874), 1670.

9. Smith, 16.

10. Ibid.

11. Von Muenchhausen, *Diary. At General Howe's Side* (Monmouth Beach, NJ: Philip Freneau Press, 1974), 31.

12. Thomas McGuire, *The Philadelphia Campaign*, Vol. I (Mechanicsburg, PA: Stackpole Books, 2006), 205.

13. Bruce Mowday, *September 11, 1777* (Shippensburg, PA: White Mane Publishing, 2002), 124; Samuel Smith, 15.

14. Harris, 288-89; McGuire, 220-21. Numerous later histories of the battle assume and repeat this inaccuracy, however, de Borre deserves criticism for other actions that afternoon.

15. Hammond, 462-67.

16. George Weedon, *Account of the Battle of Brandywine, 11 September, 1777*. Unpublished Manuscript (Chicago Historical Society).

17. This calculation is based on one soldier standing in position occupying about two feet of space. A regiment's total strength is cut in half to account for two ranks and then multiplied by two (feet) for the space its troops would occupy.

18. Mowday, 122, 4; Samuel Smith, "The Papers of General Samuel Smith," *The Historical Magazine and Notes and Queries, Concerning the Antiquities, History and Biography of America*, Vol. 7, 2nd Series, No. 2 (Morrisania, NY, February 1870), 86.

19. Mowday, 124; Harris, 190.

20. Harris, 190.

21. Gideon D. Delaplaine, ed., "The Montresor Journals." *Collections of the New York Historical Society for the Year 1881* (1882), 450.

22. Muenchhausen, 31.

23. Harris, 285; James Parker, Parker Family Papers 1760-95, Film 45, Reel 2, David Library of the American Revolution, Washington Crossing, PA, September 12 entry. It is unfortunate that more is not known about the American artillery and the details of their participation. Few accounts from them or mentioning them have surfaced.

24. Smith, *Brandywine*, 16.

25. Robert Lawson, Virginia Revolutionary War State Pension, VA 5850.

26. Michael Cecere, *They Behaved Like Soldiers* (Bowie, MD: Heritage Books, 2004), 64.

27. Mowday, 120; Cecere, 62.

28. Cecere, 63. This area has changed dramatically with modern structures, lanes, and landscaping, so it is difficult to envision the terrain, and the viewsheds, as they were in 1777.

29. Samuel Stribling, Federal Pension Application, S 37464; Charles Lander, Federal Pension Application, S 31198.

30. Jeremiah Kendall, Federal Pension Application, S 23743; Phillip Connor, Federal Pension Application, S 42134; James Arrowsmith, Federal Pension Application, W 5643.

31. Vincent Glass, Federal Pension Application, R 4059; John Neely, Federal Pension Application, W 26573.

32. Charles Ailstock, Federal Pension Application, S 1056.

33. John Perry, Federal Pension Application, S 35556; John Oliver, Federal Pension Application, S 11159.

34. David Wickliffe, Federal Pension Application, S 6409; John Matthews, Federal Pension Application, R 7023.

35. Joshua Jenkins, Virginia Revolutionary War State Pension, VA S1172; Peter Moore, Federal Pension Application, W 25716.

36. *Anonymous British Officer's Diary of the Revolution, February 12, 1776-December 30, 1777*, Sol Feinstone Collection, David Library of the American Revolution, 409-11.

37. Frederick Augustus Wetherall, *Journal of Officer B*, Sol Feinstone Collection, David Library of the American Revolution.

38. Benninghoff, 187.

39. Henry Lee, *Memoirs of the War in the Southern Department of the United States*, Vol. I (Philadelphia: Bradford and Inskeep, 1812), 16-17; Daniel McCarty, Federal Pension Application, R 5988.

40. William Scott, *Memoranda on the Battle of Brandywine and the Battle of Germantown*, Sol Feinstone Collection, David Library.

41. Mowday, 122.

42. Hammond, 464, 473.

43. Stone to Paca, 166-67.

44. McGuire, 225.

45. Hammond, 464.

46. Ibid., 575.

47. Smith, Papers, 85-86. It is difficult to determine where this lane and gateway were located. The author's opinion, based on studying the ground, historic maps, and reading the accounts is that they were to the west of the highest part of Birmingham Hill.

48. Ibid., 86. It is impossible to know where this rallying took place, but it was somewhere south of Birmingham Hill.

49. Enoch Anderson, *Personal Recollections of Captain Enoch Anderson* (New York: Arno Press, 1971), 36-37.

50. Ibid.

51. Samuel, *Brandywine*, 17.

52. Stanley J. Idzerda, Roger E. Smith, and Linda J. Pike, eds., *Lafayette's Selected Letters and Papers*, Vol. 1 (London: Cornell University Press, 1977), 94.

53. Dwight Kilbourne, *A Short History of the Maryland Line in the Continental Army* (Baltimore: Society of the Cincinnati of Maryland, 1992), 14. Panic in combat spreads with lightning speed, and one of the most difficult challenges for commanders is to rally routed troops.

54. John Boudy, Federal Pension Application, W 5858.

55. Journal of Captain William Beatty, 1776-1781, Maryland Historical Society, *Maryland Historical Magazine*, Vol. 3 (1906), 109-110; Christopher Parriott, Federal Pension Application, W 18714.

56. Jacob Allen, Federal Pension Application, R 111; Michael Palmer, Federal Pension Application, R 7899.

57. William Leard, Federal Pension Application, S 40936; Boston Medlar, Federal Pension Application, S 38212; Isaac Whiting, Federal Pension Application, R 11461.

58. Henry Wells, Federal Pension Application, S 11712.

59. Smith, Papers, 86.

60. Ibid., 462-63.

61. Ibid., 555-56.

62. Hammond, 472; "Papers Related to the Battle of Brandywine," *Proceedings of the Historical Society of Pennsylvania* (Philadelphia, 1846), Vol. I, No. 8, 53.

63. Smith, *Brandywine*, 19.

64. Hammond, 472.

65. Ibid.

66. "Diary of Sergeant Major John H. Hawkins of Congress's Own," *Pennsylvania Magazine of History and Biography*, Vol. 20 (1896), 421; Francis B. Heitman, *Historical Register of Officers of the Continental Army During the War of the Revolution* (Washington, DC: Rare Book Shop Publishing, 1914), 366. Hawkins wrote that "I lost my knapsack, which contained the following articles: . . 1 uniform Coat- brown faced with white; 1 shirt; 1 pr. Stockings; 1 sergeants sash; 1 pr. knee buckles; ½ lb Soap; 1 Orderly Book; 1 Mem. Book . . . 1 quire paper; 2 vials ink; 1 brass Ink horn; 40 Morning returns . . 1 tin gill cup; A letter and a book . . . I likewise lost my hat, but recovered it again."

CHAPTER FOUR: HEART OF THE BATTLE

1. "Selections from Correspondence, Papers of General Elias Dayton, Notes on the Battle of Germantown, with Preceding and Subsequent Movements," *Proceedings of the New Jersey Historical Society*, Vol. IX, 1860-1864. Printed at the Daily Advertiser Office, Newark, NJ, 1864.

2. Lender and Martin, 128.

3. Ibid., 127.

4. "The Journal of Ebenezer Elmer," *Pennsylvania Magazine of History and Biography*, Vol. 35 (Philadelphia: Historical Society of Pennsylvania, 1911), 105.

5. Joseph Clark, "Diary of Joseph Clark," *Proceedings of the New Jersey Historical Society* (1855), 98-99.

6. Delapline, 516, 449.

7. Harris, 293.

8. William Deakins, Federal Pension Application, S 38659; Phillip Nagel, Federal Pension Application, S 41912.

9. Rees, John U. https://www.scribd.com/document/153790118/We-wheeled-to-the-Right-to-form-the-Line-of-Battle-Colonel-Israel-Shreve-s-Journal-23-November-1776-to-14-August-1777-Including-Accounts-of-Short-Hills, 36; Heitman, 524.

10. Rees, 61.

11. Lawrence E. Babits, *A Devil of a Whipping* (Chapel Hill: University of North Carolina Press, 1998), 89.

12. Andrew Swallow, Federal Pension Application, W 61.

13. Heitman, 478; Thomas Montgomery, ed. Pennsylvania Archives, Series 5, Harrisburg, PA: 1906, Vol. 4, 508; Vol. 3, 187.

14. Invalid Pension Claims, List of Certificates for Pennsylvania, 102; John Blair Linn and William H. Egle, ed., *Pennsylvania Archives*, Series 2, Vol. I. (Harrisburg, PA: Lane S. Hart, 1880), 676, 692; Harris, 305; Patrick Hannum, "New

Light on Battle Casualties: The 9th Pennsylvania Regiment at Brandywine," *Journal of the American Revolution*, October 20, 2015. Available at https://allthingsliberty.com/2015/10/new-light-on-battle-casualties-the-9th-pennsylvania-regiment-at-brandywine/#_edn13.

15. Ibid.

16. Alexander Williamson, Federal Pension Application, S 7954; Solomon Collins, Federal Pension Application, S 39331.

17. John B.B. Trussell, *The Pennsylvania Line* (Harrisburg: Pennsylvania Historical and Museum Commission, 1993), 115.

18. J. Smith Futhey and Gilbert Cope, *History of Chester County, Pennsylvania* (Philadelphia: L.H. Everts, 1881), 79.

19. Ibid., 80. Ninety rods equals 1,485 feet.

20. J. T. Kennedy, *Map of Chester County, Pennsylvania* (Philadelphia: R. Barnes, 1856); A.R. Witmer, *Atlas of Chester County Pennsylvania* (Lancaster, PA, 1873).

21. Ibid., 80; Trussell, 114.

22. Linn and Egle, 792, 793; Trussell, 137.

23. Heitman, 540.

24. Hammond, 465.

25. Elisha Stevens, *Fragments of Memoranda Written by Him in the War of the Revolution* (Ithaca, NY: Cornell University, 1922), 6.

26. Ibid.

27. Townsend, 24.

28. Ibid., 24-25.

29. Johann Ewald, *Diary of the American War*, translated and edited by Joseph Tustin (New Haven, CT: Yale University Press, 1979), 84-85.

30. Scott.

31. Ibid., Wetherall.

32. Scott; William Dansey, William Dansey Letters, 1771-1794 (Delaware Historical Society); https://www.amrevmuseum.org/press-room/press-releases/revolutionary-era-portrait-british-army-officer-william-dansey-and-flag-he; https://www.crwflags.com/FOTW/FLAGS/us-dansy.html. Dansey captured a Delaware militia flag; either here or in the days before is not clear. The flag was green with stripes in the corner canton. It is now preserved by the Delaware Historical Society.

33. Muenchhausen, 31; Daniel Agnew, "A Biographical Sketch of Governor Richard Howell, of New Jersey," *Pennsylvania Magazine of History and Biography*, Vol. 22 (1898), 222, 224.

34. Muenchhausen, 31; "London, December 18: Extract of a letter from an Officer at Philadelphia to his friend at Edinburgh, dated Oct. 27," *Felix Farley's Bristol Journal* 26, no. 1400 (December 26, 1777).

35. Idzerda, et. al., 84, 95.

36. Ibid., 95; Heitman, 230. The sash is currently at Fraunce's Tavern in New York City.

37. Henry Stirke, "A British Officer's Revolutionary War Journal, 1776-1778," S. Sydney Bradford, ed., *Maryland Historical Magazine*, Vol. 56 (1961), 170.
38. *Remembrancer, or, Impartial Repository of Public Events for the Year 1777* (London: J. Almon, 1778), 410.
39. Delaplaine, 450.
40. McGuire, 205, 374.
41. Hammond, 464.
42. Scott.
43. Agnew, 224.
44. McGuire, 209; Harris, 314.
45. Hammond, 465.
46. *Remembrancer*, 415-17.
47. W.H. Wilkin, *Some British Soldiers in America* (London: Hugh Rees, 1914), 245-46.
48. *Journal of the Grenadier Battalion von Minnigerode*, Microfilm 232, Hessian Documents of the American Revolution, Lidgerwood Collection, Morristown National Historical Park.
49. *Reports to General von Ditfurth*, Microfiche 334, Letter Z, Hessian Documents of the American Revolution, Lidgerwood Collection, Morristown National Historical Park, 198-99.
50. Linn and Egle, 446; John Blair Linn, "The Butler Family of the Pennsylvania Line," *Pennsylvania Magazine of History and Biography*, Vol. VII (1883), 4; Trussell, 61.

CHAPTER FIVE: THE FIGHT FOR SANDY HOLLOW

1. *Ludwig Von Wurmb Journal*, Hessian Documents of the American Revolution, Lidgerwood Collection, Morristown National Historical Park, 10.
2. Muenchhausen, 31-32.
3. Marie E. and Bruce E. Burgoyne, eds., *Journal of the Hesse-Cassel Jaeger Corps and Hans Konz's List of Jaeger Officers* (Westminster, MD: Heritage Books, 2008), 14.
4. Richard St. George, "The Actions at Brandywine and Paoli," *Pennsylvania Magazine of History and Biography*, Vol. 24 (1905), 368.
5. Martin Hunter, *The Journal of Gen. Sir Martin Hunter and Some Letters of His Wife, Lady Hunter*, A. Hunter, ed. (Edinburgh: Edinburgh Press, 1894), 29-30. Hunter was later lieutenant governor of New Brunswick.
6. Reuben Lipscomb, Virginia Revolutionary War State Pension, VAS 950.
7. Jesse Sanders, Federal Pension Application, S 7440. His brother Jack later performed an important duty during the 1781 Virginia Campaign, spreading the alarm of a British raid by Banastre Tarleton on Charlottesville.
8. Leonard Shackleford, Federal Pension Application, S 6085; Levi Grooms, Virginia Land and Bounty Warrant, 1937-200.
9. Banks Dudley, Virginia Revolutionary War State Pension, VAS 1069; James Davenport, Virginia Revolutionary War State Pension, VA 8; Simon Green, Federal Pension Application, S 35987.

10. Francis Boyd, Federal Pension Application, S 42627; James Curtis, Federal Pension Application, S 39393.

11. John Malone, Federal Pension Application, S 36076; Joseph Bybee, Virginia Revolutionary War State Pension, VAS 2002.

12. Royall Lockett, Federal Pension Application, S 6799.

13. Linn and Egle, 792-93; Thomas Lucas, Federal Pension Application, S 40103.

14. Robert Mitchell, Federal Pension Application, W 7459; Joseph Garner, Federal Pension Application, W 7496; John Casey, Virginia Revolutionary War State Pension, VAS 123; Isaac Brown, Federal Pension Application, W 4415.

15. Nicholas White, Federal Pension Application, S 33898; Peter Bryan, Federal Pension Application, S 42092; Daniel Potts, Federal Pension Application, S 40275.

16. William Broughton, Virginia Revolutionary War State Pension, VAS 24; John Alverson, Federal Pension Application, S 39148; John Cordell, Federal Pension Application, W 9814; Solomon Fitzpatrick, Virginia Revolutionary War State Pension, VAS 3585.

17. Timothy O'Conner, Virginia Revolutionary War State Pension, VAS 318; Richard Taylor, Federal Pension Application, S 42039.

18. Thomas Ruter, Federal Pension Application, S 9055.

19. Smith, *Brandywine*, 19.

20. Oliver; Glover Baker, Federal Pension Application, S 10351; William Fife, Federal Pension Application, W 7265.

21. Peter Cartwright, Federal Pension Application, R 1759; John Nix, Federal Pension Application, S 30620.

22. James Kay, Federal Pension Application, S 31179; William Jones, Virginia Revolutionary War State Pension, VAS 1323.

23. David Williams, Federal Pension Application, S 4729.

24. William Moody, Federal Pension Application, S 38246; Thomas Watson, Federal Pension Application, S 17188; John Valentine, Federal Pension Application, R 10821.

25. John Bray, Federal Pension Application, W 4145; Vincent Tapp, Federal Pension Application, S 41231; Daniel Flynn, Federal Pension Application, S 39526.

26. James Ball, Federal Pension Application, W 8336; George Black, Federal Pension Application, S 6659.

27. Robert Beckham, Virginia Revolutionary War State Pension, VAS 452; James Reddin, Virginia Revolutionary War State Pension, VAS 3670.

28. William Beale, Federal Pension Application, S 37758; Joshua Younger, Federal Pension Application, W 1009; Isaac Jackson, Federal Pension Application, S 38072.

29. Cleon Moore, Virginia Revolutionary War State Pension, VAS 2307; Edward Harvey, Federal Pension Application, S 41606; James Robinson, Virginia Revolutionary War State Pension, VAS 2105.

30. Luke Metheany, Federal Pension Application. R 7149; William Metheany, Federal Pension Application, S 18122; Ludwick Miller, Virginia Revolutionary War State Pension, VAS 681.

31. Naher Norris, Federal Pension Application, R 5484. It is possible that Norris had double loaded his weapon, which sometimes happened in the confusion and stress of combat. If the surrounding noise was extremely loud, he may not have been able to hear his own weapon fire and, if it misfired, could have loaded it twice.

32. Linn and Egle, 792-93.

33. Ira Gruber, ed., *John Peebles' American War* (Mechanicsburg, PA: Stackpole Books, 1998), 133.

34. Bruce Burgoyne, trans. and ed., *The Battle of Brandywine, 11 September 1777*, 7.

35. Marie E. and Bruce Burgoyne, 14.

36. Harris, 317; Archibald Robertson, *Plan of the Battle of Brandywine*, King George III's Military Maps, Colored, Manuscript (Royal Collection Trust, St. James' Palace, London, UK). The Robertson map is crucial in understanding the battle, as it shows troop positions and terrain in great detail.

37. Harris, 318.

38. Wetherall.

39. Delaplaine, 450.

40. Richard K. Showman, *The Papers of Nathanael Greene* (Providence: Rhode Island Historical Society, 1976), Vol. 2, Report of a Court of Inquiry, Nov. 1, 1777, 188-89.

41. Weedon, *Account*.

42. Marie E. and Bruce Burgoyne, 14.

43. Ewald, 83.

44. Ibid., 85.

45. Ibid., 86.

46. Ibid.

47. Hunter, 29-30.

48. George Washington Papers, Series 6, Military Papers 1755-1798, Subseries 6C, Captured British Orderly Book, 1777-1778, loc.gov/resource/mgw6c.18_04430514/?sp=57. Several British orderly books and records fell into American hands during the Battle of Germantown in October and are part of the Washington Papers.

49. Marie E. and Bruce Burgoyne, 14.

50. "Von Wurmb, Ludwig, to Gen. Friedrich von Jungkenn, October 14, 1777," *Journal of the Johannes Schwalm Historical Association*, Vol. 6, No. 2 (1998), 10.

51. Von Wurmb, *Journal*.

52. Hunter, 29-30.

53. Marie E. and Bruce Burgoyne, 15; *Remembrancer*, 416.

54. "The Kemble Papers," Vol. 1., 1773-1789, Kemble's Journals, 1773-1789: Collections of the New York Historical Society, Vol. 16 (1883), 135.

55. Richard Cannon, *Historical Record of the Fifteenth, or the Yorkshire East Regiment of Foot* (London: Parker, Furnival, and Parker, 1848).

56. Townsend, 25-26.

57. Harris, 317; William Abbat, ed., *Major Andre's Journal* (Tarrytown, NY: 1930. Reprint, New York Times, 1968), 46.

58. Matthew H. Spring, *With Zeal and With Bayonets Only* (Norman: University of Oklahoma Press, 2008), 238.

59. Gruber, 133.

CHAPTER SIX: AFTERMATH

1. George Washington Papers, Series 6, Military Papers 1755-1798, Subseries 6C, Captured British Orderly Book, 1777-1778, loc.gov/resource/mgw6c.18_04430514/?sp=57.

2. Harris, 368.

3. Williamsburg *Virginia Gazette*, Oct. 3, 1777, p. 1 (newspaperarchive.com); John R. Sellers, *The Virginia Continental Line* (Virginia Independence Bicentennial Commission, 1978), 34; George Washington Papers, Series 6, Military Papers 1755-1798, Subseries 6C, Captured British Orderly Book, 1777-1778, loc.gov/resource/mgw6c.18_04430514/?sp=57.

4. Achilles Stapp, Federal Pension Application, 599.

5. John B.B. Trussell, *Birthplace of an Army* (Harrisburg: Pennsylvania Historical and Museum Commission, 1983), 59.

6. Ed Lengel, "New Thoughts on Valley Forge," Presentation, American Revolution Round Table, Richmond, January 27, 2021. Lengel noted that there can be a tendency to overemphasize the importance of von Steuben's reforms, and this author agrees. Keeping that point in mind, the army was gradually gaining confidence and experience, but the lack of unity in drill was a crucial factor in the defeat at Brandywine.

7. Peterkin, 7.

8. Hans Huth, ed., "Letters from a Hessian Officer," *Pennsylvania Magazine of History and Biography*, Vol. 62 (Philadelphia: Historical Society of Pennsylvania, 1938), 499.

9. Harry M. Ward, *Duty, Honor, Country* (Philadelphia: American Philosophical Society, 1979), 108.

10. Thomas G. Frothingham, *Washington: Commander in Chief* (Botson: Houghton Mifflin, 1930), 218.

11. Hammond, 462-63.

CHAPTER SEVEN: REMEMBERING

1. *Daily Gazette* (Wilmington, DE), September 10, 1877; *Daily Gazette* (Wilmington, DE), September 12, 1877.

2. Bob Guddo, *Driving Tour Information*. On file at Brandywine Battlefield Park.

3. Other examples include Civil War veterans preserving and placing monuments at the Guilford Courthouse Battlefield in North Carolina (Revolutionary

War) and the River Raisin Battlefield in Michigan (War of 1812).

4. Harris, 439-44.

5. Ibid.

6. *Report to Birmingham the Township Historic Commission*, 2010, 4-13. Available at https://www.birminghamtownship.org/history/pages/civil-war-cannons-wylie-road-and-sandy-hollow.

7. Ibid.

8. Harris, 440.

9. *Report to Birmingham Township*, 15.

10. *Strategic Landscape Preservation Plan: Rearguard Defense & Strategic Retreat*, (Delaware County, PA. 2015), 1-4.

11. https://northamericanlandtrust.org/explore/brinton-run-preserve/.

APPENDIX A: THE ARMIES

1. Hammond, 25.

2. Rees, 41.

3. Trussell, *Pennsylvania Line*, 58-59; Smith, *Brandywine*, 31; Charles Lefferts, *Uniforms of the American, British, French, and German Armies in the War of the American Revolution* (Old Greenwich, CT: W.E. Inc.), 127.

4. Trussell, *Pennsylvania Line*, 55.

5. Ibid., 88-89; Lefferts, 128.

6. Trussell, *Pennsylvania Line*, 84-85.

7. Ibid., 114-15; Lefferts, 129.

8. Trussell, *Pennsylvania Line*, 116; Hannum.

9. Trussell, *Pennsylvania Line*, 133-36; Smith, *Brandywine*, 31; Lefferts, 131; Harris, 406.

10. Smith, *Brandywine*, 31; Frank Resavy and Thomas McNichol, *Continental Army*, self published.

11. Robert K. Wright, *The Continental Army* (Washington, DC: Center of Military History, 1989), 254; Don Troiani, *Soldiers in America* (Mechanicsburg, PA: Stackpole Books, 1998), 54; Smith, *Brandywine*, 31.

12. Resavy; Harris, 406.

13. Wright, 255-56; Rees, 40.

14. Wright, 256, 257; Rees, 5.

15. Samuel Smith, 31; Harris, 172.

16. E. M. Sanchez-Saaverda, *A Guide to Virginia Military Organizations in the American Revolution* (Westminster, MD: Willow Bend Books, 1978), 38-40; Lefferts, 142; Cecere, 62.

17. Sanchez-Saaverda, 52, 30; Lefferts, 143; Michael Cecere, *Captain Thomas Posey and the 7th Virginia Regiment* (Westminster, MD: Heritage Books, 2005), 68.

18. Wright, 290; Sanchez-Saaverda, 64-65.

19. Sanchez-Saaverda, 72; Lefferts, 145.

20. Sanchez-Saaverda, 43; Lefferts, 142.

21. Sanchez-Saaverda, 55; Lefferts, 143.
22. Sanchez-Saaverda, 67; Fred Berg, *Encyclopedia of Continental Army Units* (Harrisburg, PA: Stackpole Books, 1972), 101; Lefferts, 143.
23. Sanchez-Saaverda, 74; Peter Copeland and Marko Zlatich, *General Washington's Army* (London: Osprey, 1996), 23; Lefferts, 79.
24. Berg, 93.
25. Smith, *Brandywine*, 30; Harris, 170.
26. Smith, *Brandywine*, 30.
27. Wright, 277; Smith, *Brandywine*, 30; Lefferts, 101; Harris, 406.
28. Wright, 278; Berg, 65; Smith, *Brandywine*, 30; Lefferts, 102.
29. Wright, 279; Lefferts, 104; Harris, 406.
30. Smith, *Brandywine*, 30; Harris, 406.
31. Wright, 277; Lefferts, 101.
32. Wright, 279; Lefferts, 103; Harris, 406.
33. Berg, 66; Wright, 280; Lefferts, 105.
34. Wright, 320; Smith, *Brandywine*, 30; Copeland and Zlatich, 24; Harris, 406.
35. Wright, 317; Berg, 16; Smith, *Brandywine*, 30; Copeland and Zlatich, 24.
36. Harris, 170.
37. W.J. Wood, *Battles of the Revolutionary War* (New York: Da Capo Press, 1995), 92.
38. Lengel.
39. Benninghoff, 11.
40. Ibid., 42.
41. Washington Papers, de Borre to Congress, September 17, 1777.
42. https://revwarapps.org. This website is the result of years of work by C. Leon Harris and Will Graves who have transcribed thousands of pension applications. It is an incredible resource for all sorts of research. These records were searched for soldiers who were at Brandywine, then statistics like age, education, residence, occupation, literacy, etc. were noted. In some cases these accounts contain incredible detail about the battle that are found nowhere else.
43. Edward W. Richardson, *Standards and Colors of the American Revolution* (Philadelphia: University of Pennsylvania Press, 1982), 163.
44. Ibid., 170.

BIBLIOGRAPHY

PRIMARY SOURCES

Unfortunately, there is a great lack of primary accounts from common soldiers and officers on the front lines at Brandywine. As many as could be located were used to reconstruct the events in this book. We can only speculate on the many individual experiences and emotions that happened on Birmingham Hill that afternoon and lament that a richer understanding cannot be had.

An important source used in this study is pension applications. In 1832 the federal government granted pensions to Revolutionary War veterans and their widows. The soldier, or his spouse, had to provide proof of service in the claim. Sometimes these pension records contain incredible detail not found anywhere else, yet often they are not detailed at all or have inaccuracies from clouded memories.

Abbat, William, ed. *Major Andre's Journal.* Tarrytown, NY: 1930. Reprint, New York Times, 1968.

Agnew, Daniel. "A Biographical Sketch of Governor Richard Howell, of New Jersey," *Pennsylvania Magazine of History and Biography*, Vol. 22 (1898), 221-230.

Aisltock, Charles. Federal Pension Application. S 1056.

Allen, Jacob. Federal Pension Application. R 111.

Alverson, John. Federal Pension Application. S 39148.

Anderson, Enoch. *Personal Recollections of Captain Enoch Anderson.* New York: Arno Press, 1971.

Anonymous British Officer's Diary of the Revolution, February 12, 1776-December 30, 1777. Sol Feinstone Collection, David Library of the American Revolution, Washington Crossing, PA.

Arrowsmith, James. Federal Pension Application. W 5643.

Baker, Glover. Federal Pension Application. S 10351.

Ball, James. Federal Pension Application. W 8336.

Beale, William. Federal Pension Application. S 37758.

Beckham, Robert. Virginia Revolutionary War State Pension. VAS 452.

Black, George. Federal Pension Application. S 6659.

Boudy, John. Federal Pension Application. W 5858.

Boyd, Francis. Federal Pension Application. S 42627.

Boyle, Joseph Lee. *Writings from the Valley Forge Encampment of the Continental Army.* Bowie, MD: Heritage Books, 2003.

Bray, John. Federal Pension Application. W 4145.

Broughton, William. Virginia Revolutionary War State Pension. VAS 24.

Brown, Isaac. Federal Pension Application. W 4415.

Bryan, Peter. Federal Pension Application. S 42092.

Burgoyne, Bruce, trans. and ed. *The Battle of Brandywine, 11 September 1777.*

Burgoyne, Marie E., and Bruce E. Burgoyne, eds. *Journal of the Hesse-Cassel Jaeger Corps and Hans Konz's List of Jaeger Officers.* Westminster, MD: Heritage Books, 2008.

Bybee, Joseph. Virginia Revolutionary War State Pension. VAS 2002.

Captured British Officer's Account Ledger, 1769-1771, and Diary. Washington Papers online, Library of Congress, Series 6, Military Papers, 1755-1798: Subseries C.

Cartwright, Peter. Federal Pension Application. R 1759.

Casey, John. Virginia Revolutionary War State Pension. VAS 123.

Clark, Joseph. "Diary of Joseph Clark," *Proceedings of the New Jersey Historical Society* (1855): 93-116.

Collins, Solomon. Federal Pension Application. S 39331.

Connor, Phillip. Federal Pension Application. S 42134.

Cordell, John. Federal Pension Application. W 9814.

Curtis, James. Federal Pension Application. S 39393.

Daily Gazette (Wilmington, DE), 10 September 1877.

Daily Gazette (Wilmington, DE), 12 September 1877.

Dansey, William. *William Dansey Letters, 1771-1794.* Delaware Historical Society.

Davenport, James. Virginia Revolutionary War State Pension. VA 8.

Deakins, William. Federal Pension Application. S 38659.

Delaplaine, Gideon D., ed. "The Montresor Journals," *Collections of the New York Historical Society for the Year 1881* (1882).

Diary of Sergeant Major John H. Hawkins of Congress's Own. *Pennsylvania Magazine of History and Biography*, Vol. 20 (1896), 421.

Dudley, Banks. Virginia Revolutionary War State Pension. VAS 1069.

Ewald, Johann. *Diary of the American War.* Translated and edited by Joseph Tustin. New Haven, CT: Yale University Press, 1979.

Fife, William. Federal Pension Application. W 7265.

Fitzpatrick, Solomon. Virginia Revolutionary War State Pension. VAS 3585.

Flynn, Daniel. Federal Pension Application. S 39526.

Garner, Joseph. Federal Pension Application. W 7496.

George Washington Papers. Series 6. Military Papers 1755-1798. Subseries 6C. Captured British Orderly Books, 1777-1778. loc.gov/resource/mgw6c.18_0443-0514/?sp=57.

Glass, Vincent. Federal Pension Application. R 4059.

Green, Simon. Federal Pension Application. S 35987.

Grooms, Levi. Virginia Land and Bounty Warrant. 1937-200.

Gruber, Ira, ed. *John Peebles' American War.* Mechanicsburg, PA: Stackpole Books, 1998.

Hammond, Otis G., ed. *Letters and Papers of Major-General John Sullivan: Continental Army.* Vol. 1. Concord, NH: New Hampshire Historical Society, 1930.

Harvey, Edward. Federal Pension Application. S 41606.

Henning, Walter. *The Statues at Large, Being a Collection of All the Laws of Virginia from the First Session of the Legislature, in the Year 1619.* Volume IX. Accessible at http://vagenweb.org/hening/vol09-01.htm.

Hunter, Marin. *The Journal of Gen. Sir Martin Hunter and Some Letters of His Wife, Lady Hunter.* A. Hunter, ed. Edinburgh: Edinburgh Press, 1894.

Huth, Hans, ed. "Letters from a Hessian Officer," *Pennsylvania Magazine of History and Biography*, Vol. 62 (Philadelphia: Historical Society of Pennsylvania, 1938), 488-501.

Idzerda, Stanley J. Roger E. Smith, and Linda J. Pike, eds. *Lafayette's Selected Letters and Papers*, Vol. 1. London: Cornell University Press, 1977.

Invalid Pension Claims, List of Certificates for Pennsylvania.

Jackson, Isaac. Federal Pension Application. S 38072.

Jenkins, Joshua. Virginia Revolutionary War State Pension. VAS 1172.

Jones, William. Virginia Revolutionary War State Pension. VAS 1323.

Journal of Captain William Beatty, 1776-1781. Maryland Historical Society, *Maryland Historical Magazine*, Vol. 3 (1906): 104-119.

Journal of the Grenadier Battalion von Minnigerode. Microfilm 232. Hessian Documents of the American Revolution, Lidgerwood Collection, Morristown National Historical Park.

Kay, James. Federal Pension Application. S 31179.

"The Kemble Papers." Vol. 1. 1773-1789. Kemble's Journals, 1773-1789: *Collections of the New York Historical Society*, Vol. 16 (1883), 1-250.

Kendall, Jeremiah. Federal Pension Application. S 23743.

Kennedy, J.T. *Map of Chester County, Pennsylvania.* Philadelphia: R. Barnes, 1856.

Lander, Charles. Federal Pension Application. S 31198.

Lawson, Robert. Virginia Revolutionary War State Pension. VA 5850.

Leard, William. Federal Pension Application. S 40936.

Lee, Henry. *Memoirs of the War in the Southern Department of the United States*, Vol I. Philadelphia: Bradford and Inskeep, 1812.

Linn, John Blair, and William H. Egle, ed. *Pennsylvania Archives*, Series 2, Vol I. Harrisburg, PA: Lane S. Hart, 1880.

Lipscomb, Reuben. Virginia Revolutionary War State Pension. VAS 950.

Lockett, Royal. Federal Pension Application. S 6799.

"London, December 18: Extract of a letter from an Officer at Philadelphia to his friend at Edinburgh, dated Oct. 27," *Felix Farley's Bristol Journal* 26, no. 1400 (December 26, 1777).

Lucas, Thomas. Federal Pension Application. S 40103.

Ludwig Von Wurmb Journal. Hessian Documents of the American Revolution, Lidgerwood Collection, Morristown National Historical Park.

Malone, John. Federal Pension Application. S 36076.

Matthews, John. Federal Pension Application. R 7023.

McCarty, Daniel. Federal Pension Application. R 5988.

Medlar, Boston. Federal Pension Application. S 38212.

Metheany, Luke. Federal Pension Application. R 7149.

Metheany, William. Federal Pension Application. S 18122.

Miller, Ludwick. Virginia Revolutionary War State Pension. VAS 681.

Mitchell, Robert. Federal Pension Application. W 7459.

Moody, William. Federal Pension Application. S 38246.

Moore, Cleon. Virginia Revolutionary War State Pension. VAS 2307.

Moore, Peter. Federal Pension Application. W 25716.

Nagel, Phillip. Federal Pension Application. S 41912.

Neely, John. Federal Pension Application. W 26573.

Nix, John. Federal Pension Application. S 30620.

Norris, Naher. Federal Pension Application. R 5484.

O'Conner, Timothy. Virginia Revolutionary War State Pension. VAS 318.

Oliver, John. Federal Pension Application. S 11159.

Palmer, Michael. Federal Pension Application. R 7899.

"Papers Related to the Battle of Brandywine," *Proceedings of the Historical Society of Pennsylvania* (Philadelphia, 1846), Vol. I, No. 8, 53.

Parker, James. Parker Family Papers 1760-95. Film 45, Reel 2. David Library of the American Revolution, Washington Crossing, PA.

Parriott, Christopher. Federal Pension Application. W 18714.

Perry, John. Federal Pension Application. S 35556.

Potts, Daniel. Federal Pension Application. S 40275.

Reddin, James. Virginia Revolutionary War State Pension. VAS 3670.

Remembrancer, or, Impartial Repository of Public Events for the Year 1777. London: J. Almon, 1778.

Reports to General von Ditfurth. Micorfiche 334. Letter Z. Hessian Documents of the American Revolution, Lidgerwood Collection, Morristown National Historical Park.

Robertson, Archibald. *Plan of the Battle of Brandywine.* King George III's Military Maps, Colored. Manuscript. Royal Collection Trust, St. James' Palace, London, UK.

Robinson, James. Virginia Revolutionary War State Pension. VAS 2105.

Ruter, Thomas. Federal Pension Application. S 9055.

Sanders, Jesse. Federal Pension Application. S 7440.

Scott, William. *Memoranda on the Battle of Brandywine and the Battle of Germantown.* Sol Feinstone Collection, David Library of the American Revolution, Washington Crossing, PA.

Shackleford, Leonard. Federal Pension Application. S 6085.

Showman, Richard K. *The Papers of Nathanael Greene.* Providence: Rhode Island Historical Society, 1976, Vol. 2.

Smith, Samuel. "The Papers of General Samuel Smith," *Historical Magazine and Notes and Queries, Concerning the Antiquities, History and Biography of America,* Vol. 7, 2nd Series, No. 2. Morrisania, NY, February 1870.

Stapp, Achilles. Federal Pension Application. W 599.

Stevens, Elisha. *Fragments of Memoranda Written by him in the War of the Revolution.* Ithaca, NY: Cornell University, 1922.

Stirke, Henry. "A British Officer's Revolutionary War Journal, 1776-1778," S. Sydney Bradford, ed. *Maryland Historical Magazine,* Vol. 56 (1961): 150-75.

Stone, John to William Paca, September 23, 1777. *The Chronicles of Baltimore, Being a Complete History of "Baltimore Town" and Baltimore City From the Earliest Period to the Present Time.* J. Thomas Scharf, ed. Baltimore: Turnbull Brothers, 1874.

St. George, Richard. "The Actions at Brandywine and Paoli," *Pennsylvania Magazine of History and Biography*, Vol. 24 (1905), 368.

Stribling, Samuel. Federal Pension Application. S 37464.

Swallow, Andrew. Federal Pension Application. W 61.

Tapp, Vincent. Federal Pension Application. S 41231.

Taylor, Richard. Federal Pension Application. S 42039.

Townsend, Joseph. "Some Accounts of the British army under the Command of General Howe and the Battle of Brandywine," *Eyewitness Accounts of the American Revolution*. New York: Arno Press and New York Times, 1969.

Valentine, John. Federal Pension Application. R 10821.

Valley Forge Orderly Book of General George Weedon. New Delhi: Isha Books, 2013.

Virginia Gazette, Oct. 3, 1777, 1. newspaperarchive.com.

Von Muenchhausen, *Diary. At General Howe's Side.* Monmouth Beach, NJ: Philip Freneau Press, 1974.

"Von Wurmb, Ludwig, to Gen. Friedrich von Jungkenn, October 14, 1777," *Journal of the Johannes Schwalm Historical Association*, Vol. 6, No. 2 (1998): 7-12.

Watson, Thomas. Federal Pension Application. S 17188.

Weedon, George. *Account of the Battle of Brandywine, 11 September, 1777.* Unpublished Manuscript. Chicago Historical Society.

Wells, Henry. Federal Pension Application. S 11712.

Wetherall, Frederick Augustus. *Journal of Officer B.* Sol Feinstone Collection, David Library of the American Revolution, Washington Crossing, PA.

White, Nicholas. Federal Pension Application. S 33898.

White, Samuel. Federal Pension Application. S 7871.

Whiting, Isaac. Federal Pension Application. R 11461.

Wickliffe, David. Federal Pension Application. S 6409.

Wilkin, W. H. *Some British Soldiers in America.* London: Hugh Rees, 1914.

Williams, David. Federal Pension Application. S 4729.

Williamson, Alexander. Federal Pension Application. S 7954.

Witmer, A.R. *Atlas of Chester County Pennsylvania*. Lancaster, PA, 1873.

Worthington, Chauncey Ford, ed. *The Writings of Washington*. Vol. XI. New York: G. P. Putnam Sons, 1890.

Younger, Joshua. Federal Pension Application. W 1009.

"The Journal of Ebenezer Elmer," *The Pennsylvania Magazine of History and Biography*, Vol. 35, (Philadelphia: Historical Society of Pennsylvania, 1911), 105.

SECONDARY WORKS

Babits, Lawrence E. *A Devil of a Whipping*. Chapel Hill: University of North Carolina Press, 1998.

Benninghoff, Herman O. *Valley Forge: A Genesis for Command and Control, Continental Army Style*. Gettysburg, PA: Thomas Publications, 2001.

Berg, Fred. *Encyclopedia of Continental Army Units*. Harrisburg, PA: Stackpole Books, 1972.

Briar, Marc. Personal correspondence.

Cannon, Richard. *Historical Record of the Fifteenth, or the Yorkshire East Regiment of Foot*. London: Parker, Furnival, and Parker, 1848.

Cecere, Michael. *They Behaved Like Soldiers*. Bowie, MD: Heritage Books, 2004.

———. *Captain Thomas Posey and the 7th Virginia Regiment*. Westminster, MD: Heritage Books, 2005.

Copeland, Peter, and Marko Zlatich. *General Washington's Army*. London: Osprey, 1996.

"Extracts from the Journal of Surgeon Ebenezer Elmer of the New Jersey Continental Line, September 11-13, 1777." *Pennsylvania Magazine of History and Biography*, Vol. XXV, Historical Society of Pennsylvania, 1911.

Frothingham, Thomas G. *Washington: Commander In Chief*. Boston: Houghton Mifflin, 1930.

Futhey, J. Smith, and Gilbert Cope. *History of Chester County, Pennsylvania*. Philadelphia: L.H. Everts, 1881.

Guddo, Bob. *Driving Tour Information*. On file at Brandywine Battlefield Park.

Hannum, Patrick. "New Light on Battle Casualties: The 9th Pennsylvania Regiment at Brandywine." *Journal of the American Revolution*, October 20, 2015. Available at https://allthingsliberty.com/2015/10/new-light-on-battle-casualties-the-9th-pennsylvania-regiment-at-brandywine/#_edn13.

Harris, Michael. *Brandywine*. El Dorado Hills, CA: Savas Beatie, 2014.

Heitman, Francis B. *Historical Register of Officers of the Continental Army During the War of the Revolution.* Washington, DC: Rare Book Shop Publishing, 1914.

Jackson, John. *Valley Forge: Pinnacle of Courage.* Gettysburg, PA: Thomas Publications, 1992.

Jesberger, Mike. Email to author, January 9, 2015.

Kilbourne, Dwight. *A Short History of the Maryland Line in the Continental Army.* Baltimore: Society of the Cincinnati of Maryland, 1992.

Lefferts, Charles. *Uniforms of the American, British, French, and German Armies in the War of the American Revolution.* Old Greenwich, CT: W.E. Inc.

Lender, Mark, and James K. Martin, eds. *Citizen Soldier: The Revolutionary War Journal of Joseph Bloomfield.* Yardley, PA: Westholme Publishing, 2017.

Lengel, Ed. "New Thoughts on Valley Forge." Presentation. American Revolution Round Table, Richmond, January 27, 2021.

Linn, John Blair. "The Butler Family of the Pennsylvania Line." *Pennsylvania Magazine of History and Biography*, Vol. VII (1883), 1-6.

McGuire, Thomas. *The Philadelphia Campaign.* Vol. I. Mechanicsburg, PA: Stackpole Books, 2006.

Montgomery, Thomas, ed. Pennsylvania Archives, Series 5, Volumes 3 and 4. Harrisburg, PA: 1906.

Mowday, Bruce. *September 11, 1777.* Shippensburg, PA: White Mane Publishing, 2002.

Person, Gustav. " . . . I am no advocate for blindly following the maxims of European policy." American/European Training Manuals in the Era of the American Revolution. *Continental Soldier* (Spring 2010), 10-15.

Peterkin, Ernest. *The Exercise of Arms in the Continental Army.* Alexandria Bay, NY: Museum Restoration Services, 1989.

Resavy, Frank, and Thomas McNichol. *Continental Army.* Self published.

Rees, John U. https://www.scribd.com/document/153790118/We-wheeled-to-the-Right-to-form-the-Line-of-Battle-Colonel-Israel-Shreve-s-Journal-23-November-1776-to-14-August-1777-Including-Accounts-of-Short-Hills.

Report to Birmingham the Township Historic Commission. 2010. Available at https://www.birminghamtownship.org/history/pages/civil-war-cannons-wylie-road-and-sandy-hollow.

Richardson, Edward W. *Standards and Colors of the American Revolution.* Philadelphia: University of Pennsylvania Press, 1982.

Russell, T. Triplett, and John K. Gott. *Fauquier County in the Revolution*. Westminster, MD: Willow Bend Books, 1988.

Sanchez-Saaverda, E. M. *A Guide to Virginia Military Organizations in the American Revolution*. Westminster, MD: Willow Bend Books, 1978.

"Selections from Correspondence, Papers of General Elias Dayton, Notes on the Battle of Germantown, with Preceding and Subsequent Movements," *Proceedings of the New Jersey Historical Society*, Vol. IX, 1860-1864. Printed at the Daily Advertiser Office, Newark, NJ, 1864.

Sellers, John R. *The Virginia Continental Line*. Virginia Independence Bicentennial Commission, 1978.

Smith, Samuel. *The Battle of Brandywine*. Monmouth Beach, NJ: Philip Freneau Press, 1976.

Spring, Matthew H. *With Zeal and With Bayonets Only*. Norman: University of Oklahoma Press, 2008.

Strategic Landscape Preservation Plan: Rearguard Defense & Strategic Retreat. Delaware County, PA, 2015.

Trussell, John B. *The Pennsylvania Line*. Harrisburg: Pennsylvania Historical and Museum Commission, 1993.

_____. *Birthplace of an Army*. Harrisburg: Pennsylvania Historical and Museum Commission, 1983.

Ward, Christopher and Leon DeValinger. *The Delaware Continentals*. Wilmington: Historical Society of Delaware, 1941.

Ward, Harry M. *Duty, Honor, Country*. Philadelphia: American Philosophical Society, 1979.

Wood, W.J. *Battles of the Revolutionary War*. New York: Da Capo Press, 1995.

Wright, Robert K. *The Continental Army*. Washington, DC: Center of Military History, 1989.

ONLINE SOURCES

https://www.amrevmuseum.org/press-room/press-releases/revolutionary-era-portrait-british-army-officer-william-dansey-and-flag-he

http://allthingsliberty.com/2014/05/the-25-deadliest-battles-of-the-revolutionary-war/

https://www.crwflags.com/FOTW/FLAGS/us-dansy.html

http://memory.loc.gov/ammem/gwhtml

https://northamericanlandtrust.org/explore/brinton-run-preserve/

https://revwarapps.org

https://storymaps.arcgis.com/stories/9cef8b93eaa94faf8e106edbb737ef1c

https://newspaperarchive.com/williamsburg-virginia-gazette-oct-03-
    1777-p-1/

https://www.usgs.gov/core-science-systems/national-geospatial-pro-
    gram/topographic-maps

ACKNOWLEDGMENTS

THANKS TO Andrew Outten and Brandon Miller of Brandywine Battlefield Historic Park, Melissa Weissert of the National Museum of the US Army, Marc Brier of Valley Forge National Historical Park, Eric Olsen of Morristown National Historical Park, Bruce Venter, William Welsch, and Mark Lender of the Revolutionary War Round Table in Richmond, Dr. Lawrence Babits, researcher Michael Cecere, Mike Jesberger of the 1st New Jersey reenactment group, author Michael Harris, German translator John Dunlap, author Doug Crenshaw, reenactor and researcher Bryan Brown, reenactor Steve Santucci, copy editors Kate Gruber and Nate Best, cover designer Trudi Gershenov, and publisher Bruce H. Franklin. Bob Yankle generously provided some great photos. Tom King endured me babbling on about this battle and was willing to go on a fifteen-mile hike to explore the site. As always, Sarah Nance supports me in everything I do, *thank you*.

This work would not be possible without the tremendous work of transcribing pensions by C. Leon Harris and Will Graves. I admire their dedication and achievements.

INDEX